SARAH,

As you grow always
set to express that
unique spirit that
is you ... Off the Beat

Enjoy!

[signature]

ENDORSEMENTS

Jerry Busone knows leadership—in basketball and in business. His integrity, values, and focus on people have enabled him over the years to recognize talent, develop leaders, and build unstoppable teams—both on and off the court. Read *Off the Bench Leadership* and learn how to create a winning culture in your organization.

—KEN BLANCHARD
Coauthor, *The One Minute Manager*®
and *Legendary Service*

Jerry Busone is one of the experts in business leadership and motivation. I was fortunate enough to work with him at the start of my leadership career, and the skills he taught have helped shape the leader I am today. He gave me much to pass on to my teams over the years. This is a book you definitely want to read to take yourself and teams to the next level.

—ALAN GUROCK
Group vice president,
North American commercial analytics sales, Adobe

Jerry Busone was an integral part of one of the great stories in sports history—the ascension of the Old Dominion University women's basketball team to the top of the national rankings. They were pioneers in women's athletics. Busone recalls the lessons he learned—and taught—as a coach and makes them relevant to the business environment. Bottom line: it's a game plan for success.

—JIM DUCIBELLA
Author, *King of Clubs: The Great Golf Marathon of 1938*; columnist,
Virginia Golfer; web writer, College of William and Mary

We live in a time of great change and arguably much of what we know about leading today is becoming obviated, which is why *Off the Bench Leadership* is such a helpful contribution to every leader's arsenal. It embraces a shift from industrial models to a model for the 21st century from a successful basketball coach and corporate sales leader. Packed with great stories and tons of practical advice from both worlds, *Off the Bench Leadership* is a radically fresh road map to infuse innovative change into leading teams. Pure magic. Read and enjoy.

—RON HUBSHER
Author, *Closing Time: The 7 Immutable Laws of Sales Negotiation*
Managing Director, Sales Optimization Group

Off the Bench Leadership provides direction for planning as well as a strategic understanding of your values, which can give you the drive, determination, and decision making needed to have the courage to act.

—CHRIS BURLEY, SR.
Director Learning and Performance, ADP

The common trait in all the great leaders I have known is the eager willingness to jump up and jump in. It's to jump up "off the bench," to use my gifted cousin's phrase, and get things done. None are content cheering from the bench.

Thinking back on my family and Jerry's, I saw our fathers join with their wives to raise eight wildly different but enthusiastically motivated leaders. They grew us into educators, coaches, business leaders, a celebrated chef, an inspired folk artist, and a highly praised and beloved musician. What we all share is the blessing of having parents who showed up, got involved, and would not stand for life on the sidelines. The enviable successes that my cousin Jerry has had in education, sports, business, motivational training, and now writing is a tribute to his courage and hard work.

Please know that the book you are about to read is the result of Jerry's heart, soul, sweat, nerve, immense courage, and a lifetime of learnings, both business and personal. But there is one thing more. Jerry is lifted daily by his enthusiastic embrace of life. All of the Busone cousins have this gift. We love the good, the bad, and everything in between about living and we are not at all shy about sharing that love. That is for me perhaps the single greatest indicator of leadership. Jerry possesses this in abundance; he has since he was a boy. He has much to share with all of us.

—PHILIP BUSONE
Partner, Wilson Jill Associates Staffing Services

Since my first encounter with Jerry as a candidate for the vice president of sales position for ADP's Central Florida Region, I have been a champion of his mission to serve and lead others. In selecting Jerry as a leader, I knew his passion for teaching, modeling behavior, planning to win, and doggedly driving for team wins would be the right formula for success. With expectations from every direction—the forty associates and managers, his peer group, and headquarters—it was clear the expectations he had for himself were far greater than the sum of all the others.

Jerry relocated from California, dove head-first into the role, and thus began a new chapter by taking a team to heights they had never dreamed of, including winning ADP'S Employer Services Region of the Year a short two years later. Jerry earned respect and unrivaled loyalty from his team while building a national awareness and support for his style, substance, and techniques. With ADP, Jerry has instilled an extraordinary belief in thousands of sales leaders and associates that achieving what may seem impossible is possible.

—MITCHELL TOUART
Business Development and Solutions, Knowledge Universe

Jerry Busone assumed the leadership of our Boston region sales team at Intuit during 2002. Before Jerry arrived, we were the worst performing sales team in the entire country. Within a year, we rose to become the top performing sales team in the country. Jerry empowered us to believe in ourselves, strengthened our internal bond, and inspired us to execute our sales game plan daily. Jerry put us in a position to win. Jerry is the Bill Parcells of sales leadership. Off the Bench Leading works.

—JASON MAXWELL
President, MassPay

During my twenty-one years with ADP, Jerry Busone was one of the most charismatic leaders I worked with. His selfless and inspirational style of management set Jerry apart from the rest of the pack. Indeed, he truly cared about his people, and in turn, they trusted him and performed to their highest ability. You will be moved by Jerry's insights and up the caliber of your game after reading this book.

—BOB WHITTEMORE
President, AOA Consultants

Jerry, thank you for helping me to focus off the bench, on the things that really matter as a sales executive. Although my number didn't look pretty during the first quarter, working with you allowed me to check in and make sure I was spending my time on the right things. You helped me avoid "the noise" and it worked! We started to see the fruits of our labor in quarter two and have been looking down at our number ever since.

—CARYN LEE
Sales executive, ADP, major accounts

For anyone who desires to lead, *Off the Bench Leadership* is an easy read, full of inspiring words from a proven leader.

—MIKE KUPIEC
Private and public sector manager

Jerry's approach to leading teams and inspiring people to reach their full potential transcends both the locker room and the boardroom, and really hits home in the living room. Jerry is a "people coach" who has personally brought out the best in me as an athlete, a businessman, and a father.

—KEN POWELL
Vice president, global marketing and sales productivity, SunGard

Jerry was the sales manager who would always help everyone. When you had a bad day, he would greet you with a big smile and then find some way to help you see it as a great day. This was over twenty-one years ago, but you always remember the great people.

A bonus of social media is staying in touch with the positive people we meet in all our periods of life. And when Jerry started his website and blog, he started sending out "gifts of wisdom" that were an email inbox highlight. His book is just the next step.

Off the Bench Leadership should be a must read for anyone who manages or wants to manage, but anyone will benefit from learning how to be a better person, sibling, parent, friend, and spouse.

—MICHAEL C. WALES II
Senior sales consultant

In *Off The Bench Leadership*, Jerry Busone demonstrates how a successful career is simply a decision away. Coach Jerry's personal story of boldly veering from his predictable and comfortable life path inspires and instructs. Everyone from emerging to senior leaders will find this book useful and enjoyable.

—SEAN O'NEIL
Principal, One to One Leadership; author, *Bare Knuckle People Management: Creating Success with the Team You Have— Winners, Losers, Misfits and All*

Jerry Busone has mastered the art and science of bringing out the best in people, and now he is sharing the recipe for his secret sauce. His practical, engaging style does for the reader what Jerry does for all of us: creates a simple path forward to little changes that deliver big results.

—AMY CRAWFORD STEWART
Senior vice president, marketing and sales strategy,
One Call Care Management

Off The Bench Leadership is an extraordinary book that gives you great insight on what leadership truly is. Jerry paints the clear picture that leadership is not just mere words; it's about getting your hands dirty. If you are in need of a makeover when it comes to leadership, read Jerry's book today.

—KORY MINOR
Former NFL linebacker; author, *Make A Touchdown Of Your Life: 24 Keys to Crossing the Goal Line of Success;* founder, Elite Leadership Academy

Jerry introduced me to individual employee development. He taught me to address the individual, highlight their strengths, and help them exploit those strengths. He also taught me you can lead a horse to water and you can entice them to drink through personal motivation, articles, and stories to inspire their souls. Through these techniques, he took our team off the sidelines and not only put us in the game, he made us winners.

—LEE ANN HOLLINGTON GEHERS
Vice president, client relations, ARI

OFF THE BENCH LEADERSHIP

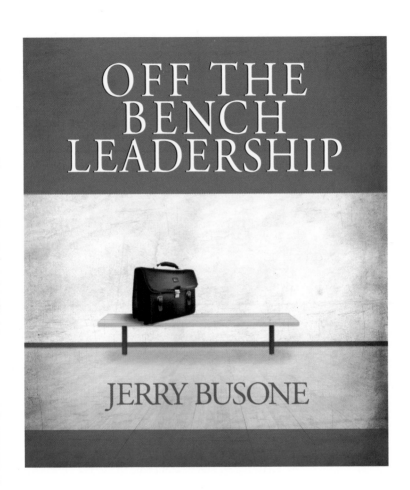

JERRY BUSONE

BroadStreet
P U B L I S H I N G

BroadStreet Publishing Group, LLC
Racine, Wisconsin, USA
www.broadstreetpublishing.com

OFF THE BENCH LEADERSHIP:
Be Better Than Your Best

ISBN-13: 978-1-4245-4946-7 (print book)
ISBN-13: 978-1-4245-4953-5 (e-book)

Cover and interior design by Garborg Design Works, Inc. at www.garborgdesign.com

Typesetting by Katherine Lloyd, www.TheDESKonline.com
Edited by Stephanie Sample

Stock or custom editions of BroadStreet Publishing titles may be purchased in bulk for educational, business, ministry, fundraising, or sales promotional use. For information, please e-mail info@broadstreetpublishing.com.

Printed in China

DEDICATION

First and foremost, this book is dedicated to my daughter, Carly. From the moment she was born, she gave me a reason to get up every day. Through our journey—the good and the bad—Carly inspired me to keep going. Now grown with a family of her own, she continues to be a guiding light in my life. Of all my accomplishments, she is the most extraordinary. Carly, I'm proud to be your dad.

To my parents, who gave me the foundation to know what it means to live life to the fullest. They dedicated each day to creating a better life for our family and like all great leaders, they showed us the way. My parents taught me the value of doing much with little, and I owe my will to succeed to them. They are the original Off the Bench Leaders.

To my brothers, Joe and Anthony, who have always accepted me for who I am, a life-long dreamer. They lived the wins and losses and never stopped believing in me. They were my safety net, freeing me take the risks I did. To them and their families, I say thank you for keeping our traditions alive.

Finally, I dedicate this book to every emerging leader I've connected with. You inspire me every day. I root for your success.

CONTENTS

FOREWORD

It was the fall of 1978. I had just been hired to my first, real, big-time broadcasting position: Sports Director of WTAR Radio in Norfolk, Virginia. A big part of my job was to broadcast college basketball for the hometown team, the Old Dominion University Monarchs.

Just before the season began, the general manager of the station announced that we would not only carry the men's games, but that WTAR, the dominant AM radio station in Hampton Roads, would also broadcast women's basketball games featuring the Lady Monarchs, a first for a station that big anywhere in the United States.

That's how I met Jerry Busone, ODU's life-of-the-party assistant coach for the women's team. The Lady Monarchs were in their glory, with national championships led by the legends of women's basketball: Nancy Lieberman, Inge Nissen, Anne Donovan, and coached by the highly successful Marianne Stanley.

It's not easy being an assistant. You are there to serve at the pleasure of the head coach, while cultivating your own relationships with the players, their parents, school administrators, and sometimes, the radio announcer.

But it was there that Jerry started formulating his leadership foundation, the essence of which is contained in pages of *Off the Bench Leadership*.

One of the great differences between sports and business is the scoreboard. It is very easy in sports to see at the end of the day whether you won or lost. Not only is it displayed on that scoreboard, but it's also in every newspaper, website, and app the instant the final horn blows. It's not so easy in business to see if you are winning and losing day by day.

But by using the wisdom on these pages, you will be able to judge for yourself and your team if you are moving toward victory on a moment-by-moment basis. It takes hard work, discipline, and practice—traits that coaches and athletes use on a daily basis.

Those traits are easily transferrable from basketball to business.

This is your playbook, the outline for unlimited success.

Now get off the bench and lead.

—Bob Rathbun
TV Play-by-Play, Atlanta Hawks & Philips Arena

Chapter 1

OFF THE BENCH LEADING FOR EMERGING, NEW, AND EXPERIENCED LEADERS

*Every member of the team—leaders and players—
must exhibit an off-the-bench mind-set and habits in
order for the team to win.*

Eleven seconds to go. The Old Dominion University (ODU) Lady Monarchs were behind by one point. This would be a defining moment, one way or another.

The scene was crazy. We were at University of Tennessee facing Pat Summitt—one of the most admired and celebrated coaches in the game. We had just enough time to dial in one last play. Coach Marianne Stanley quickly settled the team down, and we decided to run a play to Inge Nissen, our All-American center, using fellow All-American Nancy Lieberman, our player of the year. They executed the play flawlessly, tying the game. Inge was fouled during the play, so it all came down to a free throw. Swoosh. We came out of Knoxville with a 74–72 win.

Our real competition that night wasn't Tennessee; it was finishing in second place. The kids, the team, and the coaching staff were united. We were not going to accept the clichés "Better luck next time," or "It's not whether you win or lose…"

I heard someone say that finishing second is like finding a fly in your soup. Who wants that? The Lady Monarchs knew from experience that anything less than first wouldn't feel right. As a team, we all agreed second was not an option. That night, our coaching staff came metaphorically off the bench to help secure the win. A winning culture was imbedded into the team early on, and the team executed when it mattered. We would go on to win back-to-back national championships and three straight Final Fours.

Marianne only played for the national championship, and our collaboration taught me to play, coach, and lead at another level. This is where the foundation for Off the Bench Leading was born.

What if…you had the chance to bring extraordinary success to yourself and your teams?

What if…that success could lead you to a place you've only dreamed of?

And what if it only took a mind-set and the decision to give a little bit better than your best to get there? Would you sign up for that?

Fast-forward to 1992 and my first sales team in Ontario, California. We had nine people, and eight were brand new. Not surprisingly, we got off to a slow start. As the team started to gel, we went on a good run. With the fiscal year winding down, we were close to making our team goal, and eight out of the nine team members were close to making their individual goals as well.

It was time for one more play. I came "off the bench" to

increase the urgency, change the cadence, and drive them to the finish line. They dug in and executed flawlessly, and the team went on to President's Club, a company honor only bestowed on an extraordinary few. The winning culture had been established, and the team wouldn't settle for anything but a win.

In our fast-paced, ever-changing global marketplace, it is no longer acceptable to lead from the nosebleed section. You have to be ready to come off the bench—every day. Otherwise, you cast chance to the wind. Frontline leading in Corporate America is the toughest role to succeed at, but it is absolutely essential. To make an impact on the team you lead, you have to get out there and work side by side with them.

Off the Bench Leading is about defining and developing what's great about the people you lead. This requires patience and practice. In sports, you practice a ton to play the next game. You don't get that luxury in business, yet you still have to win. The only hope for today's leaders is to get out of the office—off the bench—and to collaborate with their teams.

This book is for anyone who's currently leading and wants extraordinary success. This book is also for emerging leaders looking for an edge. I'll show you how to lead from off the bench and contribute to your team in a fresh, effective way. I speak not just from experience, but also from the highest level of success in both athletics and business. Having learned from some of the most remarkable leaders and coaches in their respective areas, I'll share my journey—from coaching championship basketball teams to leading high-level sales teams. You may be surprised by how similar the roles actually are.

Off the Bench Leadership is dedicated to regular men and women, just like myself, who want to affect people's lives and achieve success in today's workplace. My off-the-bench principles come from real-life workplace experiences and observations regarding the little things that make the extraordinary, extraordinary. While the individual strategies are not entirely new or solely my own, I've combined and refined them into a unique style: Off the Bench Leadership.

In each chapter, you will find four consistent elements to help you as a leader:

- Off the Bench Leadership strategies and principles.
- Stories from the front lines that I trust will bring the principles to life.
- A section at the end of the chapter called "Get in the Game," which contains actionable ways you can put what you've just read into practice.
- A short summary of the key points of the chapter in "Coach's Corner."

I've spent years cultivating and developing emerging and new leaders while helping the tenured ones stay fresh. I have a passion to help those living this every day. Helping others and seeing the impact an Off the Bench Leader can make is what drives me. It is my sincere wish that this book will help you be a little better than your best self and that you—and those you lead—will emerge greater than ever before.

BELIEVE TO SUCCEED

Chapter 2

DREAM YOUR WAY
TO SUCCESS

*Top performers in sports and business start their day
with a dream or vision, then go and accomplish it.
You own the success you lend to others daily.*

By the time I reached the Chesapeake Bay Bridge tunnel on
my way to Norfolk, Virginia, and Old Dominion University,
I had driven more than fifteen hours and eight hundred miles. All
along the way I kept telling myself: *Dream big. Act big. This can be
done. Don't quit.* I had one goal: National Champions. I pictured
how it would lay out and how I would celebrate over and over.
Never mind I didn't know the players; I was simply going with
the gut feeling I had about the head coach who hired me. Over
and over, I reminded myself who I would become: a National
Champion.

Everyone I knew wanted to know why I would uproot
myself and leave everything behind. Why would I move into a
tiny apartment in the roughest part of Norfolk? Inevitably, every
conversation came down to a few questions: Where the heck is
ODU? What is ODU? "Tell me again," they would say. "After all

the hours you've spent studying, practicing, and building a successful career, why are you choosing to start over?"

Furthermore, why wouldn't I want to follow everyone else and get a job working for the state of New York? After all, they offered great benefits, a pension, and a good salary. Why move to a place where no one knows me and to a college few people have even heard of?

My life as it stood was not luxurious by any means, but it was safe. I was a high school business teacher and basketball coach at Catholic Central, coaching the girls' and the freshman boys' teams. I became a big fish in a little pond; we won a lot of games, thanks in large part to my fabulous mentor, varsity coach Don Bassett. Coach Don took an interest in me and taught me the game inside and out. I was truly a student, and I owe him a debt of gratitude I can never repay. The success he helped me achieve is what gave me the courage to dream big enough to eventually move on.

Inspiration—from the Nosebleed Section

Living my nice, comfortable life, I never really thought about what else was out there. I was raised by parents who had little education and a great work ethic. Where I grew up, you got a job close to home, found a nice girl to marry, then settled down nearby and showed up every Sunday for family dinner. It really was a great life. I was happy. But then my perspective changed— on a spontaneous trip to a baseball game.

In the summers, I did small jobs in the community, like working for the parks and recreation. School was not in session; I took the opportunity to study for advanced degrees and played in a summer league, but I still had a fair share of time on my hands. Sitting around one lazy, hot summer day, my friends and I got the urge to drive to New York to see the Yankees play. We were more than three hours away, but we were young and inspired—so we went for it. We had taken a lot of short day trips to the lake, local events, and even to Saratoga, but we'd never gone as far as New York City.

We arrived at the stadium and bought the only tickets we could afford: out in right field, all the way at the top, literally the cheapest seats in the house. Even up there in the proverbial nosebleed section, it was wonderful. I love the look of a well-manicured stadium, and the history there was palpable. I'd been to Yankee Stadium with my dad when I was younger, but this was just my friends and me, ready to enjoy some evening baseball with a hot dog and a beer.

As the game went on, we talked and talked. One of the things I love most about baseball is that it's such a social game. There is no expectation of silence. A huge part of the fun is the conversation in the stands, about the game and everything else. My buddy Dave said, "Isn't it amazing that all these guys are doing what they love? They are living their childhood dreams." It hit me at that moment: up until then I was watching life from the nosebleed section of the stadium. I wanted to take in the big game from the sidelines, right on the field. I wanted more.

Then and there, I made a promise to myself to get in there, dream big, and make every moment count. It was then that I began to explore the possibility of coaching at the college level. It was then that I threw myself into working summer basketball camps, driving long distances to get there week after week for little or no pay. I didn't care. I loved the game, and I was following a dream. I was off the bench.

At one of those camps, a chance meeting with two of the most influential and talented coaches I ever met, Cathy Rush and Marianne Stanley, changed my life forever. That connection eventually led to an incredible offer from Marianne to be her assistant at ODU. With that offer and the faith it represented in my ability and passion, Marianne did more than give me a change of scenery. She elevated my dream. I went there not just to become a coach at the college level. I went there to win a national championship.

Dream Big, Life Is Short

How about you? Are you watching life from the top of the stadium, or are you on the field? Are you making most moments count? Do you have a big dream that weighs on your "what if"? Let's be real: life is short. Average life expectancy is between seventy-six and eighty-one years.[1] That's a blip on the radar. And corporate life? The average corporate job lasts just 4.4 years.[2] So why not take charge and make every moment count?

Life is about playing full out, all the time, with passion, compassion, and enthusiasm. It's about doing what you love and finding love in what you do. We have to get in the game now and make this week count. The first step off the bench is finding out what—and where—*your* dream is.

You don't have to have a grandiose plan; I could easily have lived a dream right where I grew up. There is nothing that says you have to actually *go* anywhere to achieve your dreams. For me personally, I had to move on in order to find the "more" I was looking for. I am challenged by chasing my dreams, but that's me. The most important thing is to make sure you *have* dreams.

23

Ignore the Doubters

Whatever you dream of, whether it's hitting a lofty sales goal, winning a national championship, or pulling off an aggressive makeover at work, you will find people who will doubt you. People will tell you it's impossible. Whatever you try to do "full out," there will be naysayers. I definitely had mine. When I told everyone what I wanted to do and why, at first they thought I was joking; then they thought I was insane. "You're not going to an unknown school and winning a national championship," they said. "Your family is here; your life is here; everyone knows you here." I didn't listen; I knew I had to go. My desire to get off the bench and reach for an aggressive challenge—my belief that I could realize my dream—was how I'd gotten the job. People said that I was crazy, that I was throwing my life away, and that it was impossible.

Possible is just a word people use to justify what they have or where they are in life. *Possible* is another way to say, "I'm not changing." Why? Because it's a whole lot easier to accept what you have in life than to go out, disrupt your balance, and make a difference. It's how we settle for what's handed to us: our job, our family, our territory, our quota, our work assignments. And that's okay for many, but Off the Bench Leaders play for the big prize. They don't listen to the doubters. They help their teams achieve more than they thought they could by dreaming big and expecting everyone else to, too.

Keep It Real

As an Off the Bench Leader, you will want to bring your team to goals they don't believe are possible. As someone who has spent my career doing this, let me caution you: ground your dreams in reality. Know the odds, and identify potential roadmaps to success. Who has done what you hope to do? How did they do it? If it's never been done, what has to happen in order for you to be the first? You can dream all you want, but if it's not grounded in data, facts, and assessed opportunity, it's likely going to stay just that— a dream. As a leader, you first have to sell your team on the idea that nothing is impossible." After that, make sure you give them the "roadmap to the stars" or a plan to implement the dream.

I'm not telling you to go out and disrupt your life, territory, quota, or job like I did. There is a personal price attached to any big change, and those decisions need to be carefully weighed. Be realistic about what you are able and willing to risk or even sacrifice. What I *am* telling you to do is look outside what you have right now, just a little bit; elevate your dream. Elevate your team's dream. Then make it happen.

Impossible? Never!

The impossible is only so until someone does it for the first time. Consider the telephone, the first train, flying people all over the world in a few hours, landing on the moon and coming back safely, having thousands of songs and photos in your pocket, and watching TV wherever you are. All of this was impossible until the first person dreamed it, and then they and their team made it happen. Don't be afraid to be first. Dream the dream, invest in the goal, and promote it daily.

Humor me for a second. Place one hand on top of your head and the other over your heart. The only thing holding you, or any

Off the Bench Leader, back from extraordinary success is the distance between your two hands. What you need to succeed is the dream in your heart and the belief, skill, and drive in your head. Own it. Invest your heart in it. It is not impossible.

Have you written your dream down? There is a highly successful vice president of sales in St. Louis whose leadership and team's accomplishments I greatly admire. I asked her about her goals and dreams once, and she told me she has them written out. She keeps them near her bathroom mirror so she will see them every day. A daily visual reminder of your objective goes a long way toward making it happen. And I love the bathroom mirror idea. It forces you to look yourself right in the eyes and say, "I'm doing this. We're doing this."

So what happened at ODU? Did my impossible dream pay off? In our first forty games, the Lady Monarchs were 36–4. They went on to three Final Fours, winning two of them. They went to a National Invitation Tournament and won, and they came within one basket of a fourth Final Four. There were three All-Americans, several retired jerseys, several Olympians, and Coach Stanley was named Women's Coach of the Year by Association for Intercollegiate Athletics for Women (AIAW). They set attendance records and were the first women's college basketball team to be nationally televised.

Impossible? No way. Just don't ask the naysayers. My extraordinary history was written one dream at a time, by taking on tough assignments as a coach, sales leader, and leadership development executive. Over and over I've seen, in my own life and in the lives of others, that with a dream, foundation, and follow-through, nothing is impossible.

Get in the Game

Right now, today, take a look at your situation. What do you want? Make a list or take inventory of what you currently have. Assess your current reality and then assign a goal to it. Now stretch the goal; go beyond what you think is possible. If you are currently leading a team, where is the biggest, best place you can take them? If you are still working toward your first leadership role, start observing the job you aspire to. Get involved in a leadership development program. Find a mentor and start asking for assignments, pieces of their job, to test and prove yourself. It's never too early to begin branding yourself as the next leader.

Dream big, but do a reality check by road mapping the goal in reverse. Identify the activities it will take to get there and the support you will need. Leaders, assess your current people; do you need more talent on your team? How about your resources; are there tools you don't currently have that are vital to your plan? How can you acquire them? You have to believe it with all your heart to sell it to your team, so do the research.

Emerging leaders, what stands between you and your dream? This is where you have career conversations with your boss and with their boss. Understand where you fit in. What do you have to do to get to the next level? With your boss, develop and agree upon a checklist of tasks to perform in addition to your current job. Never assume there won't be movement and opportunity; things change all the time.

Now own it. Write it down. Write it down for yourself, and write it down for your team. Bring everyone who works with you into your plan so they will believe it too.

COACH'S CORNER

- Don't watch from the sidelines; go get your dream!

- Belief is what separates impossible from possible.

- Have a plan; create a reverse road map from the finish line.

- Draw a visual and post it where you and others can see it.

Chapter 3

CONVINCE YOURSELF YOU CAN

People who are confident are happier, feel better about themselves, and rise to the next level of performance. At the very least, pretend you're confident. You just may fool yourself.

Picture yourself living and working in a beautiful city with perfect weather. You have a great boss and are part of a terrific team. You've done nothing but succeed since you arrived. Life is pretty much perfect. Insert wrinkle: the president of sales wants to sit down and discuss your career.

Several years after I left coaching for corporate sales, I found myself eating breakfast on a patio at a beautiful hotel overlooking the ocean. I was nervous, not sure what to expect. I knew I wasn't in trouble, but I also had a feeling things were about to change. We started with small talk, and I noticed he was taking notes in a rather large notebook. He said, tongue in cheek, "Look at this view! You really have a tough job."

I was nervous enough to completely miss the point and began to defend my turf. He laughed and said, "Hey, how rough can it be? You drive to work with the ocean on your left, and when you come home at night it's on your right." It was true. Except for Hawaii, Santa Barbara is as close to paradise as I've ever been.

He asked me what I wanted from my career and, to be honest, I didn't really have an answer. I hadn't thought long term, but I did mention I had my eye on the next level, VP for a sales region. I asked what opportunities were out there for me, and he shared his catch phrase: "The jobs and opportunities you will aspire to haven't even been created yet." I took that message to heart, unaware of just how true it would be for me.

Next, he asked me what I thought about Florida. I answered honestly and told him I had never given Florida much thought one way or the other. Then I found out why we were having breakfast on this lovely terrace. He thought I was the right guy to go out and turn around an underachieving region. I told him I'd speak to my family and friends and get back to him.

Pretty much everyone was focused on reminding me I had a great gig in Southern California, and they were right. But the Off the Bench Leader in me wanted to take a risk. I'd experienced enough success to be confident it was the right move, and also, I just couldn't resist the challenge. Decision made: it was off to Tampa.

Fake It 'til You Make It

Prior to the current outgoing VP who was moving on to a new role, the Tampa office had, as I heard a senior executive say, the worst history in the company. Welcome, new guy; my job was going to be a tough one. I immediately got busy hiring, surveying, and observing behaviors all around me. How could I convince a place with very little prior success to reach for and hit the moon? I had told them we would be tops in our space, but I didn't have a clear vision of it yet. I took the advice "fake it 'til you make it" to heart and decided to figure it out on the fly. Sometimes that's the way you have to roll.

All eyes were on me. *Who is this guy? What does he want? Can I trust him?* I'm sure that's what was going through everyone's head. I was "the guy from the left coast," not the in-house candidate. The team of leaders I had to work with consisted of mostly women, which was good for me. Having coached women's basketball for so many years, I felt very much at ease with them.

I devoted a good deal of time to understanding the turnaround and the opportunity before us. I met with each manager individually, and I made a strong connection with two in particular. Janet was a high-producing, highly motivated sales executive, and Lee Anne was a rookie with tremendous potential and drive. They would turn out to be my guiding coalition and the driving force behind the job ahead of us.

Defending Our Turf

The new quota assignment under my leadership represented a significant increase over all their previous goals and achievements. I was puzzling out how we'd hit the numbers and, even harder, how I would sell my vision to the teams. I had to infuse some high-octane fuel into this group, bring in some fun, and build their confidence along with mine.

And then it happened. I learned the annual President's Club celebration for top producers was to be held, for the first time ever, in Orlando. This was a gift. The trip was usually to Europe or Hawaii, but someone looked down on me and chose Orlando and all it had to offer. Thank you, Mickey Mouse. They even included a private concert with Elton John, making the reward that much sweeter.

I now had a big dream and the perfect theme to take to the managers in hopes of gaining their support. We would not let anyone else step up on stage as the top region in the country, not in our house. We would go to war to defend our turf. We would "Take Back Central Florida." I was particularly passionate about the theme because it played perfectly into my strength as a coach. My confidence was starting to soar; now I needed data and the numbers to bring the managers up there with me.

The sales executives bought in, so then we had to convince our key folks—our sales people—that they could achieve the grand goal. We mulled it over as a management team for some time, even going off site for long planning sessions. We came off the bench and decided to take a huge risk, one that would pay off even bigger when we pulled it off.

Believe It, Then Achieve It

The sales reps had to set their own goals. They had to be given the opportunity to define their territory, their quota, and the ultimate number they would achieve. Keep in mind this was 1999; there was no territory optimization or development software to rely on. But I knew in my heart, after all those years of coaching, that if they believed they could do it, they would. If they bought in and developed the mind-set that they were in a fight to defend their territory, they *would* hold on to it. "Nobody celebrates in our house but us" would become the prevailing attitude.

We took the risk; one by one, we met with every sales person and had them tell us what territory they wanted and what quota they would hit. There were no options, no excuses, and no exceptions. Make a choice and own it, we told them. Believe we will be the top team in the country. There was no Plan B. Meanwhile, I also met with the four sales managers. I got them into a room and had them write out quotas for every person in the area, without knowing who would be assigned to them. They had to believe everyone could succeed.

The result? The sales reps came in with collective quotas that were 35 percent above their own targets, and the managers came back with 25 percent higher quotas. Getting them to believe they could do the impossible was going to be easy now.

When I announced the rollout and assigned the quotas, I saw exuberance, engagement, and a highly motivated team. The trust built in that process and the confidence they felt carried throughout the year. They went out and not only crushed the numbers, but they achieved the distinction of best sales team in the country. Just like we'd dreamed it, they went on stage, on their own "dirt," and took back Central Florida—for good. That area today is three times as large, and they consistently deliver, year upon year.

It's amazing what people can accomplish when they believe in themselves. I also saw it happen at my first job, coaching girls basketball at Central Catholic. My belief in myself and in them is how I convinced them they would be a ranked team in New York State. They chose to believe me and gained the confidence to win fifty-five games to two losses. Later, at the University of Hawaii, the women's basketball team made it to their first post-season tournament, regardless of the fact no one thought they could do it—except them. Believe in your people, provide the right environment, and execute the right plan—then watch them amaze you.

Get in the Game

Any time you move to a new position, you need to be the most confident person in the room. Whether it's your first or your fifth leadership role, dig in and show confidence, even if you don't feel it, until you figure things out. "Fake it 'til you make it" may sound funny, but it's been proven to work. It is easier to act your way to feeling than the other way around.

Convincing yourself first is not pie-in-the-sky thinking. Most of that conviction should come from planning and doing your homework. Take inventory of your team, your market, and your opportunity. The work you do behind the scenes is no different than putting a game plan together. When you look ahead at a season, gather and pore over all the data you can access. Take advantage of the fact that you can answer almost any question in a matter of seconds from your smartphone. Consider the best- and worst-case scenarios, then figure out how you can maximize the best case. This boils down to, simply, "How will you win?"

As an Off the Bench Leader, believe in yourself first, then believe in your people and announce to the world, "We are and will continue to be the best at what we do." Support it with a rally cry or theme; build a culture of confidence by working toward a common goal. Whether you are an emerging, new, or advanced leader, you should take stock in this fact: engaged people fly higher.

Nothing builds your confidence like success. Put yourself and your team in the best possible position to win at every turn. Take advantage of the ready availability of data, and use it to form achievable plans. Create opportunities for small wins along the way by breaking down your goal into smaller steps.

Going in with a solid plan is ideal, but let's face it, the world is moving fast. Circumstances change, markets change, and we all know people can change on a dime. Sometimes the best-laid plans need reworking. When things get messy, don't give your confidence away. Your team should not see a difference in you no matter what you are facing. Be the consistent, confident force in your workplace. Simply refuse to give in to the voice that says you can't.

Coach's Corner

- Be the most confident person in the room. "Fake it 'til you make it."

- Do your homework. Convincing yourself you can requires planning.

- Believe in yourself first, then believe in your people. They'll only believe if you do.

- No matter what happens, don't give your confidence away.

Chapter 4

KEEP THE POSITIVES IN PERSPECTIVE

*You are what you think, so don't let what
you don't have keep you from focusing on what
you do have. The thoughts you choose allow you
to embrace greatness or welcome mediocrity.
When adversity pushes at you, push back.*

Imagine going from a situation where on your worst day, you still had a shot to win and on your best day, you blew the other team out of the water. Imagine leaving that environment for one where on your worst day, you were blown out and on your best day, you only lost by ten points. Really, imagine it. Without a relentlessly positive mind-set, you would never survive. That was my situation.

Moving from coaching basketball to business sales had its ups and downs, to say the least. I had days that were so hard, I'd find myself sitting in my car on the side of the road asking, "What were you thinking?" It was rough, and it took all my willpower to keep the negatives from taking over my mind-set. I actually thought about resigning a couple of times and returning to coaching, but a mentor and boss, Paul Silitsky, helped change my perspective when he gave me some of the best advice I've ever received.

Following a string of particularly bad luck in the field, I went to Paul and said, "You know what? I may not be cut out for this." Paul knew the wisdom in getting out of your everyday environment to help you see the big picture, so he took me to a beach in Belmont Shore, California. As we breathed in the salt air and watched the waves, he said, "You can't win every week, and you will have setbacks. You will always have ups and downs; I fight them every day. So at the end of the day, ask yourself these questions: Do the good things you have outweigh the bad? Have you done all you can to be the person you want to become, and not just who you are today?"

You Own You

What I learned—the thing that struck me so deeply—was this: You are what you think. You ultimately control how you feel about yourself. Over time, the thoughts you choose to dwell on allow you to choose, and to embrace, who you become. Don't miss this; it's right at the core of Off the Bench Leadership. *You own you.* You decide who you want to be, and that requires keeping the positives in perspective, especially in the face of setbacks. I left coaching for business sales because I wanted the challenge, and because I *knew* I could do it. I just had to remind myself.

This is not easy for me to share, but I think it's important. I've had bouts of depression my entire life. I remember Mom helping me through a really tough spell back in high school, and on a couple of occasions after I was on my own, my parents were concerned enough to come to where I was living to help me through.

They were my rocks, and I leaned on them. People who love you are a well of support when you need to be reminded of all that's good in your life.

Over time, I've learned to focus exclusively on the good, keeping the positives in front of me and leveraging small wins in whatever I do. It also helps me immensely to stay fit, both mentally and physically. It's amazing what thirty minutes on the elliptical can do for your perspective. Believing in something bigger than yourself is also a huge help: I get a great deal of comfort from my faith—talk about seeing the big picture. I own me, and I choose to be positive in every aspect of my life.

Just Look in the Mirror

Maybe you are a rockstar salesperson who on your worst day hits your plan and on your best day blows out your quota. When storms and fires come, and they will, remember who you are. Handling adversity from the perspective of always winning takes work. It means never forgetting what got you where you are. Look in the mirror. You are a star; you just had a bad day (week, month, quarter…) Push back, refuse to cave to negative thoughts, and bring your best attitude to the work place.

As an Off the Bench Leader, there is nothing more valuable you can give to your team than to spread this attitude. Many of my teams became the best in their game at one time or another, and in most cases, their success continued well after I was gone. I always tried to be the guy *holding* the mirror, showing them all the good happening around them. I'd like to believe those reflections of their best moments helped drive the success they achieved. They are what

I value most from my career: the "band of brothers and sisters" who are still out there, living, working, and succeeding every day.

One Possession at a Time

You can find a lot of good if you just attack today. In sales, it's simple. My first vice president, Ralph Canape, taught his people at the end of every day to look back and answer two questions: "What appointments did I set?" and "Who did I see that could advance my sales?" Focusing on small sections of an entire goal is a good method for keeping all positives in perspective; if you are moving forward, you are creating positive momentum.

In basketball, my mentor Don Bassett always said to take the game one possession at a time: "Stop them on defense, go down the court, and score. That's one. Do it again. That's two. A game is about winning more possessions than the other team." Leading is like that too. Focus on one possession at a time, and observe every small victory.

Susan Scott, author of *Fierce Conversations*, echoes the sentiment by reminding us we succeed or fail one conversation at a time. Think about that. It becomes very manageable to keep the positives in perspective by breaking your goal down into doable parts. A successful sales call. A productive conversation. Off the Bench Leaders keep a positive mind-set by handling their days, months, and years one possession, one conversation, at a time.

Change the Message

I know a story of a sales VP who took over a new area and hired consultants to come in and do research on the opportunity before him and his team. When the consultants came to share their findings, he was having a regional meeting with all of his sales managers. Excited for the future and certain the results were positive, he told the consultants to proceed with all the managers present.

Things did not go as expected. According to the research, there was not a great opportunity. In fact, by all likelihood the region would be hard pressed to reach any lofty goals. "Historically," they said, "this area does not do well." The new VP found himself facing what you might call…a challenge. The message from the consultants wasn't good, but that didn't have to be the message the leaders brought to their teams. They enhanced the message, turning the lack of history into a challenge, and they focused on the talent and determination of the team to create a new history.

Fast-forward a year. That sales group had a banner year, meeting all of their goals and even exceeding them in a few cases. They hit numbers no one thought possible, achieving what had never been done before. Remembering the results from the research group, everyone wanted to know how they did it. "What changed?" they wanted to know. The leader replied, "It was tough; we couldn't change the data, so we changed the message."

There Are No Mistakes

Jazz legend Miles Davis once said, "Do not fear mistakes; there are none." I embrace that. We need to look failure straight in the eye and see what good we can pull from it. For me, getting back up after a tough week is fun. A new week is just that—new. After learning what you can from the mistakes of last week, choose to start fresh. Give adversity a swift kick into oblivion. Banish self-pity, drop the excuses, and do something positive.

To truly embrace this mind-set, you have to commit. No options, no exceptions, no excuses. You have to live it, and that's a lot easier said than done. We all face challenges every day, from negative feedback to unexpected setbacks. No one is truly secure, and it takes work to maintain the right attitude day after day. Obstacles pull at us throughout our lives; the trick is taking them on and pushing back.

Push Back

A powerful sales conference I once attended had the theme "Be Bold." I kept that message with me. Boldness requires a positive attitude, but more than that, it demands that when tough challenges arise—when you fall, or whenever adversity is pushing at you—your job is to push back. I know it's not what we teach our kids and with good reason, but as a leader, when you get knocked down it's not enough to simply get back up. You have to move forward, and that requires pushing back. You have to say no to negative thinking; push it away. Your thoughts define you, and you cannot let a problem, a missed workout, a blown deal, or even tragedy determine who you are. Boldly focus on the good. It's always there; sometimes you just need to look a little deeper to find it.

There is a lot of good happening. Recognize it, leverage it, and use it to push back against your difficulties. Be bold, and you'll quickly realize you really can be what you think.

Get in the Game

To create a positive off-the-bench culture, meet with people one on one. Find out what they expect from you and what, if you meet those expectations, you can expect from them. Keep this relatively simple; have a list of three things. Ask them what their toughest failures were, find out what challenges them, and ask what keeps them up at night. Then open a line of communication so they know you are there to help them through it.

Ask people regularly, "What's good for you right now?" Keep them thinking about it. Do the same for yourself; focus internally on what's good in your world right now, this very moment.

Look at and address constructive criticism immediately; there is always something good in there to build on.

"Leaders are readers" is a great little quote. Using part of your day to read is important, even if it's for just a few minutes. Leverage periodicals, find white papers online, and be on the lookout for great stories. There is much written about overcoming obstacles and staying positive; use what's out there to build up your own outlook and pass it onto others.

Assess your outlook. Do you take the time every day to capture the best of what you did that day? If you do, keep it up. If you don't, start today.

Observation, evidence, and specifics sell people on ideas. Your ideas should be reinforced by data, but remember: data alone will not sell an idea, and the data doesn't always tell you what you want to hear; you need a positive message.

Find people that live positively at a high level, and let them guide you, especially on the tough days. Rely on your friends, your family, your network, and a higher power for sources of positivity when you are struggling to keep your perspective.

Failures and setbacks are part of life. Manage them by focusing on what's good right now. As soon as the storm comes, turn your attention to everything you have going for you. As an Off the Bench Leader, you can head off many potential problems before your team even knows they exist.

Sometimes, despite all your effort, you cannot overcome a series of failures and stay where you are. If this happens, tie up your loose ends as well as possible, then move on and find a place to reinvent yourself. If you focus on all you have going for you, you can make a comeback.

COACH'S CORNER

- You control the thoughts that define you.

- Take every task, every day, one possession at a time.

- When challenged with a setback, be bold and push back.

- Keep yourself and your team focused on the positives. Ask, "What's good for you today?"

- There really is no such thing as failure. If you cannot overcome a negative, move on, reinvent yourself, and make a comeback.

YOU
OWN YOU

Chapter 5

BE THE TRUE YOU

*Be true to yourself, be honest with others,
and be the same person everywhere you go.*

I get asked two questions all the time: "Why did you leave ODU for Hawaii?" and "Why did you leave coaching?" Neither has a simple answer. My career at ODU was great, but in order to be true to myself, I had to acknowledge this truth: a thirst for the next hurdle in life is what propels me. Always has, always will. We had some unbelievable seasons, experiencing the kind of success that fulfills dreams. But then I needed to step out and see what kind of impact I could make in a completely different scenario. I was ready for new dreams. That's just who I am.

There were other factors too: I didn't aspire to be a lifetime head coach; I was interested in administration and ultimately wanted to lead a department. I also wanted to complete my master's degree, which required an internship. For these reasons and more, Hawaii made sense. Still, leaving ODU was hard.

To say my first foray into the world of Division I women's basketball coaching was a challenge is an understatement. We were young, inexperienced, and in many ways just working on growing up. We were pioneers, trying to make a name for ourselves and women's basketball in general and attract fans. Then there was the fact that I am a guy; men in the sport weren't the most revered at the time. However, Coach believed in me and it worked for us.

I have never felt more valued at a workplace than at ODU. Through the good, the bad, and even a little bit of ugly, Coach Stanley and Dr. Jim Jarrett hung by me. I value my time there more than any other. ODU is where I grew the most. I made and learned from many mistakes, I shaped and was shaped by some truly amazing people, and ultimately I developed into the person I am today. The risks we took, the mistakes we made, and the people we befriended all played a role in how we matured. But like I said, I'm always looking ahead to the next challenge.

Take the Hurdle

We had just finished a successful season at ODU, and I was contemplating and assessing my career path. I could have stayed at ODU another year, and maybe I would have. But then I received a note from University of Hawaii asking to speak to me about a head coaching position. I was not interested in the least, but my wife said, "Why not take the trip and see? At the worst, you still got to go to Hawaii."

So we went. Cindy, the women's athletic director, had a great program outline. The men's director, Stan Sheriff, was a former NFL player. I met everyone involved with the program, as well as the team. I connected with the kids, and something touched me. They wanted a great program and a strong coach. And they had a strong desire to win. I'd often wondered what it would be like to take a ragtag team and give them life. Was this my chance?

We returned to Virginia, and I took some time to consider the move from every angle. At the end of the day, I knew I was finished at ODU. In order to be true to myself, I had to take on this challenge. I accepted the position, and I believe it's where I did the best coaching of my career. We didn't have the biggest talent, but what we did have was the biggest group of overachievers I've ever worked with. I've never regretted taking that hurdle. It showed me what was possible.

Listen to Yourself

In Hawaii, I learned I could definitely coach. I knew I could gather and recruit talent and assist as I had at ODU, but my inner self was challenging me to take on another impossible assignment. People said, "Win? In Hawaii? Not happening. You can't get great players to go there; it's too far." Fair enough, but I knew something they didn't: I knew myself. Under no circumstances would I accept defeat.

The team was small and fast. The coaching staff consisted of myself and Suzanne Woolston, who had played for ODU. She came out to study and try her hand at being an assistant coach. She excelled at both. What we lacked in size and talent, we made up for in heart and execution of fundamentals. In just two short years, we did it. The team made it to post-season play, and the stands started to fill in. People were coming to the games.

The risk I took when I listened to my true self opened doors for the coaches and players who followed, and the program flourished. When you're consistently you, everyone you touch benefits.

Live the Truth

When leading off the bench, you are freed to be your authentic self. You don't have to live two lives, one as the image other people create for you and one as who you really are. In fact, it's a huge mistake to do so. As a leader, remaining—or getting back to— your true self will drive your team's success.

Moving into my first role in a Fortune 500 company was mostly about learning to operate and understand who I was in Corporate America. It was tough coming from a whole different arena, but I was determined to prove I could succeed at business and remain my true self. Did I make mistakes? You bet I did; I made many. That's part of the beauty of Off the Bench Leading: learning from your mistakes.

When I took on my first leadership assignment, I thought back to my days coaching basketball. I thought of the drive I had, the focus I created, and how I was always striving to be better than my best self. Those things weren't unique to coaching. They were unique to me. They were the truth. That was how I needed to operate in order to be my authentic self. I wanted to impact the people I worked around, to help them grow and achieve their best. I wanted to add value to the company. The best way to do that? Just Jerry being Jerry.

People whose lives you touch won't always remember the scores, the awards, or even the trips. Sure, those things are great, but what they remember most is what you said to them. How did you make them feel? How did you inspire them? I recently asked a group of my former players and sales staff to share some of the

"Jerryisms," as some of my personal catchphrases have come to be called, that they remembered. Much of what they shared was funny, and several times I found myself thinking, *Did I really say that?* You know what, though? They all got it. Years later, they respected the way I remained true to myself and never gave them anything but reality.

One former sales representative said, "When you first came in, telling it like it is and pushing us, we thought you were crazy. But after being around you, we knew you always had our best interests at heart. We learned to appreciate the candor." I was my authentic self, living and telling the truth.

Be Honest and Be You

Candor is a key missing ingredient in many of today's teams and conversations. If you are going to be true to you and your team, you have to be frank in your conversations. The number-one thing I get asked to train on is how to effectively have a difficult conversation. At the risk of stating the obvious, people don't like to have difficult conversations; they're uncomfortable. Because of that, it can be tempting to sugarcoat the message. Don't do it. If you've been leading off the bench, the people around know who you are. This makes the task simple, really: be honest and be *you*. If you are a tough, no-nonsense leader, you'll lose credibility if you suddenly deal with them with kid gloves.

I learned this lesson early in my business career from a good friend, Bob Moisa, as he helped me gear up for a crucial uncomfortable conversation. I had to tell one of my sales reps he was going to lose a large sale, one that would have earned him an award, due to a policy mistake. He was one of my best people, and I lost sleep wondering how he would take the news.

Bob said, "These conversations are a fact of business. Whatever you do, think twice, then speak once, and you'll be fine." That formula, thinking twice, led me to realize that in every interaction we'd had, I'd been authentic around that sales rep and all my reps. He knew who I was. He knew he could trust me to tell him the truth. This helped me deliver the message sincerely and succinctly. Sure it still hurt, but hearing the news from someone who was consistent made the message more palatable. It always does.

Get in the Game

Earn the right to communicate honestly by being authentic. Take a few minutes from time to time and consider who you are, who you want to be, and how you are perceived by others. Your effectiveness as a leader lies in how people perceive you. Do their impressions line up with your own?

The best leaders I've ever been around are tough, but fair; they can push their people, ask hard questions, and help people laser focus on objectives, because their teams know what to expect.

What conversations have you been putting off? Are there any messages you need to deliver but are reluctant to? Tough and difficult messaging is a fact of life as a leader, and putting it off does no good for either party. Think twice, then say it once.

I know I don't have to tell you that Off the Bench Leading cannot take place behind a closed door. It happens *out there*. It's about showing your true self to each person you touch and being the same person in the field as you are inside your four walls.

COACH'S CORNER

- When you're consistently you, everyone you touch benefits.

- You don't have to be two people. Just be you, all the time.

- Speak with candor.

- Think twice, then speak once.

Chapter 6

GET ALONG WITH MANY

*Trust and approachability are the keys
to workable and successful partnerships with
everyone you come in contact with.*

A struggling sales leader came to me for coaching. He had
seven people: five were new, and the other two were senior
salespeople. I asked right away if he'd leveraged the senior leaders
as mentors, and he replied, "Not really; I don't have them come
to team meetings because they're senior. One is a good friend
of mine, and we connect on the weekends from time to time. I
pretty much let them do what they want."

I thought for a moment, then asked him, "If it came down to
it, could you fire your friend?" He said, "I hadn't really thought
about it, but now that you've asked, no. I don't think I could."

Imagine how the other people on the team must have felt.
Imagine the lack of trust such a relationship created among the
other team members. People are smart; they have no trouble
connecting the dots to see that one person has a much closer connection to the boss. No wonder the team was struggling.

And let's not forget his failure to leverage his experienced staff to help him develop the new team members. They were a tremendous asset and completely underutilized. He could have saved himself quite a bit of time, not to mention established some much-needed respect and rapport, had he set up those mentoring relationships.

Don't Try to Be Superman. Or Wonder Woman.

Being able to get things done through other people is essential to a leader. Can you imagine a head coach trying to be successful without assistants, scorekeepers, and university support? In today's business climate, there is simply no way you can do it all yourself. Getting "off the bench" to help your team does not mean going out and doing their jobs for them. That's playing Superman or Wonder Woman, and it's a sure way to burn out.

Pick just about any company in America, and you can look at two leaders and see an example where one thrives and another fails. Look more closely at the successful leader. I'll bet they're off the bench, making sure the people around them all connect. I'll further bet they are trusted and respected, that they are clearly established as the leader of their team. This person allows channels to drive the business, relying on each person to perform a necessary role.

Now let's look at the leader who didn't make it. Here you'll see a good performer and hard worker, someone who did all the right things on paper but failed to connect with their people and create a culture of trust. Rather than developing and relying on established channels, they tried to do it all. Because they hadn't established any relationships, they were kept busy putting out fires, most of which could have been avoided if they'd been more collaborative and inclusive. They became the proverbial "chicken with its head cut off" and inadvertently sent a message to the team that a leader who wants to survive never wants to send: "I don't trust you to do your job." Trying to be Superman or Wonder Woman and control everything is the death of many a leadership opportunity.

Balance: the Midas Touch

The primary difference between the two leaders in our example is the presence—or lack—of a trusting environment and a network of collaborative partners with clearly defined roles. People who are treated as underlings, or perceive themselves as underlings, don't typically feel valued enough to rise up to, let alone exceed, expectations. People who see themselves as equal to or even superior to their boss will also not give their best to the team. The key is balance. Getting along with many requires both a respectful, supportive climate and a clearly defined line between a leader and their team.

I know of a CEO who is very approachable and is sincerely interested in what's going on around him. He invites and welcomes feedback and gives it honestly and respectfully. He is never too busy to say hello, even going out of his way to make visitors feel valued and welcome—not something that falls under the job description of a Fortune 500 CEO. Leaders like this tend to have the Midas touch wherever they go. They care and collaborate enough to make everyone feel genuinely important, but it is always clear the relationship is based on business.

I also know of leaders who take feedback personally, so they don't reach out to those who have the pulse of the company. They are so deep in their own convictions that they cannot see the long-term impact their narrow outlook has on their business.

It Takes a Village

A leader has to immediately and clearly define relationship boundaries with the people who report to him. You want and need great chemistry, but you also need to draw a line between influencing and collaborating with a team while still being able to handle conflict and maintain your position as leader. It's an admittedly fine line, and one that seems to get blurrier all the time. However, it's absolutely critical. Being relatable and likable is key, but without appropriate boundaries, the culture of trust fails to form.

One of the toughest things I witnessed in my career was leaders being removed from their roles. Why would a leader not live up to their potential? After working long and hard to get noticed, branding themselves as leadership material, and doing everything possible to be considered for a promotion, then interviewing for and winning the job, why do so many new leaders become disengaged and discouraged?

The first place to look is at the relationships the leader developed during their time at the helm. "It takes a village" may be cliché, but that's because it's true. You need a full 360-degree support network, from work to home and everything in between. And you must understand the difference between professional friendship and personal friendship.

As human beings, one of our basic instincts is to establish

close relationships with the people around us. We have an innate desire to be liked, and this can result in trying to be everything to everyone, all the time. It's especially common in the instance of promotions from within a team, where friendships have already formed and now suddenly, one person is in charge. It's so common, in fact, there's a name for it: buddy to boss syndrome. A new leader mistakenly equates being liked with being trusted and respected. It's a dangerous mistake. You need a village to get things done, but remember: every village needs a mayor.

Execution over Emotion

Care and influence and inspire, but keep it about the business. It sounds like a big con, doesn't it? It sounds like you only pretend to genuinely care about your people. Think of it this way: as a basketball coach, no one gets closer to your players than you. On the teams I coached, we cared for every player deeply and had a vested interest in her college career. However, we couldn't base our decisions about the lineup on those feelings. The ultimate goal, winning, was always top of mind; we had to play the best players for any given situation to put the team in a position to win, regardless of personal feelings. We didn't hesitate to bench someone who wasn't getting it done, no matter how much we liked her.

Likewise, consider a favorite teacher or college professor; you knew you had a rapport, and you could even imagine being friends once you were no longer student and teacher, but when the term paper was due, you, like everyone else, knew who was in charge. They had expectations of you, and you had to deliver.

This applies to any number of relationships in your day-to-day life: housekeeper, dentist, lawyer, the person who plows your driveway after a big snowstorm, and on and on. Throughout our lives, special connections form. We come to care for these people, but if they fail to execute within their role, you end the business relationship.

Hire People You'd Invite to Dinner

This principle, Get Along with Many, trickles into hiring. As someone trustworthy, trusting, and approachable, an Off the Bench Leader builds a team of like-minded souls. For myself, that means I want to hire people I would be proud to have at my family dinner table. I choose to partner with people who see the value in chasing goals as part of a collaborative team. Give me people who hate to lose as opposed to those who only love to win. Give me the "fight-from-behind group" rather than the frontrunners.

As social beings, we need close, supportive connections with others. And let's face it. Your coworkers are the ones who get most of your time. Friendships are going to happen. Many members of my early teams, even back to my first team out of college, stay in touch at least once a year. This means the world to me. The best compliment a leader can get, even beyond being lauded for great results, is when people who have worked for you stay in touch after one of you moves on. No amount of awards can replace genuine human connection.

Ask for and Accept the Truth

If there's one thing that sets all leaders apart, it's how open they are to the truth. The ability to create an organization that feels safe for people to speak up and give feedback is what separates great leaders from the rest. Off the Bench Leaders know they need to understand what's going on in their world and also to have a clear picture of their own effectiveness, so they surround themselves with people who will tell them the truth. It's difficult in this century to run a business on data alone, yet many leaders have a hard time accepting honest feedback. It's easy to become narcissistic, especially if it's your first real time in the spotlight. Instead of seeking out and acting on honest feedback, insecure leaders surround themselves with people who cover the truth and paint over reality in order to gain favor.

I've seen leaders go down simply because they didn't know how they were perceived by their teams. I've seen leaders who, as key people left all around them, would not look into the underlying reasons they were losing their top performers. Truth is not nice to have; truth is a staple in any organization planning for sustainable success. Numbers don't tell the entire story.

Trust Is a Must

Right now, take a moment and think of the person who has had the most profound impact on your life thus far. When you get that person in your head, think of and list their attributes. What did you come up with? I'll bet somewhere high on that list is trustworthiness. I had the opportunity to take in a talk by Lou Holtz, former head football coach at the University of Notre Dame. He said that when someone meets you, they are thinking three things: Who is this person, what do they want, and can I trust them? Trust is not nice to have. Trust is a must.

Conflict Is Inevitable

An Off the Bench Leader constantly assesses performance and ability, and based on those assessments, motivates people to grow. Sometimes this means telling someone to change a behavior or an attitude. This is a time when your relationship must be all business. Friends accept you "warts and all," but a leader must facilitate change when necessary. If the relationship is built with boundaries, warmth, and trust, they'll accept the feedback and act on it enthusiastically.

I think it goes without saying that virtually no one enjoys conflict. Inevitably, a leader will have to diffuse tension, referee disputes, and occasionally disrupt people's lives. Perhaps the toughest day of any leader's career is the first time they have to let someone go. If that thought doesn't bother you, or if you've already fired people and you enjoy it, you should not be leading teams. Compassion is a nonnegotiable essential.

Get in the Game

Getting off the bench means you genuinely care about your people and they can see that. You spend a huge chunk of your lives together, and that time is considerably more rewarding when there is genuine appropriate friendship.

Remember your relationship with your team exists in order to accomplish a common worthwhile goal. The Off the Bench Leader never loses sight of their ultimate purpose and is able to place that purpose above their personal feelings.

As the leader, you must know when to develop, when to

nurture, and when to put the brakes on the relationships you foster in the pursuit of success for the team.

Keep sight of the importance of building trust. Do this by being honest, open, and consistent.

Go beyond the data. Make it safe for your people to speak with you, and seek out those who know the heartbeat of your organization. Yes, you need a great quota to shoot for, but you also need to surround yourself with people who will share real-time feedback. Once you have all the information—once you know the whole truth—soak it all in. Then do what needs to be done, especially if you learn you need to make a change.

How comfortable are you addressing performance issues with each person on your team? How readily could you deliver a tough message? Identify relationships that need work, either with closeness or with establishing boundaries, and take appropriate steps.

Be compassionate, but do what needs to be done. If you are too tentative about discipline and give too many concessions in order to maintain harmony, it will hurt your credibility as a leader. Ask yourself, "If anyone on my team made a mistake that warranted termination, could I do it?"

Consider a person you trust completely. Emulate that person's qualities.

COACH'S CORNER

- There is only one Superman, only one Wonder Woman, and it's not you. Involve the whole team.

- Find and stay on the right side of the line between buddy and boss.

- Build your business friendships around reaching a common goal.

- Be approachable. Ask for and accept the truth about your own effectiveness.

- Conflict is inevitable. Approach it with conviction and compassion.

Chapter 7

HAVE FUN OR
FIND IT ELSEWHERE

Life should be fun and so should your career.
If the job ceases to be fun, move on or find joy
in something else. We have only rented time on
this earth, so share it with those you care about most.

I grew up, like most people, in a regular house with regular family values. My Italian family had pride and a great work ethic; it was important to my parents that we learn the value of hard work, gratitude, and finding joy wherever we could. Dad was a great guy, but not very empathetic: you got a bad grade, you fixed it; you got hurt, you played through it. He was all about getting up after a setback and finishing well. The man worked on a factory assembly line for twelve hours a day, sometimes six days a week. For him, happiness came from knowing he was doing all he could to give his family the best.

My mom had a true servant's heart. She raised and picked up after three kids, putting a hot meal on the table every night. That's impressive on its own, but Mom did it while working two jobs. She found great joy in showing hospitality to guests, always cooking extra so we'd be ready for unexpected company. Whenever that surprise knock came on the door, and it came pretty often, Mom was ready. It was her pleasure to entertain, no matter how busy she was. She also brought plates to friends who were ill or laid off, and sometimes she'd just run a meal over to the neighbors. Holidays around our house were a picture out of a magazine; Mom loved to set a table that dropped jaws. Service and entertaining were her passion. It was fun for her.

Responsibilities are part of life, but so is enjoyment. Mom and Dad modeled this in their daily lives, and they made every effort to help us find our own outlets for fun and happiness. I was sent to dance lessons, piano lessons and the like, but none of that really clicked and I quit as as soon as I could. While my dad didn't encourage quitting something once we'd started, he also believed there was value in trying things, in learning what you don't love. When something is really not for you, it's better to quit than to do it unhappily ever after. Once they started putting me in sports, I found my passion.

They didn't know it at the time, but everything my folks did prepared me for my turn on the court. From a very early age, they showed me that I owned my happiness. It took years and a lot of trial and error to really sink in, but Mom and Dad planted the seed: love what you're doing, or go somewhere else. And whatever you do, enjoy the people you are blessed to have in your life.

Follow the Joy

It comes down to this: Off the Bench Leading won't take you anywhere unless you love what you do. Most of my life I've gotten that right, which means I've moved around a lot in order to reach the self-actualization I enjoy today. Everything is in sync; work, life, and spirit integrate seamlessly; to put it simply, I love everything. I love people, and I love coaching. Putting the two together and seeing the impact I can have on their lives is what gets me out of bed every morning.

This would never have happened if I hadn't been committed to happiness—to combining my passions, gifts, and opportunities into a truly meaningful life. When things weren't right, or when there was no more joy, I went out to find it again.

In my professional life, the first time I moved toward fun and joy was at a small basketball camp in the Poconos. I was coaching high school hoops, and had gone there to work with one of my players. All week long, I witnessed hundreds of young athletes and coaches practicing their skills and perfecting the game they loved. It was there I first met Marianne Stanley, one of the most influential people in my life. Her work ethic, passion, and focus on being the best inspired me so greatly, I left my comfortable life and joined her coaching staff at ODU.

She clearly loved her job, and she expertly balanced home with work. This was no small feat, as she was a single mom and the head coach of a Division I basketball team with high hopes of gaining national recognition. Regardless of what might be happening behind the scenes, Marianne always came to work with a smile on her face.

I wanted that too. All of it. The nationally ranked team, the absolute love of what I did, and the smile that never seemed to leave my face. So I went for it; I followed the joy. And I haven't stopped chasing it yet.

Follow the Road Map

Doing what you love may lead to periods of uncertainty. I know I was uncertain at the beginning of my sales career, but I was following a passion for conquering the seemingly impossible, something that is fun for me. The path to success and enjoyment contains a fair share of risk. It's scary to move on, but if you feel yourself being tugged in a new direction, and if you don't love where you are right now, go for it! After you settle in, the fun that comes from working in your strengths and passions will follow.

If you've made a move toward a job you love and it's not happening quite yet, commit to follow the road map, to wait for the payoff. It's important to focus on what makes you happy about your work, especially since the whole thing can't possibly be fun. We enjoy—or don't enjoy—our lives by choice. Knowing the final destination is where you've always wanted to be helps you survive the ups, downs, and dramas along the way.

Life should be fun and so should your career. Everyone deserves to enjoy the way they spend their days and nights. There will be tough times, but if you love what you do, you will be able to stick it out and believe in the future.

If the job totally ceases to be fun, if you lose your passion, do something else. Follow a new map. Because, truly, there is no substitute for passion. It's what fuels you each day.

It's a Great Life. Really.

A classic chronic workaholic, for many years and through multiple job changes, I worked and worked and worked, thinking that was how life was. You slaved to provide for the family, and then you fit them in where you could. I kept trying different ways to integrate my life more, but it wasn't until I lost my marriage that I learned it was possible to actually enjoy my job and my family and to have adequate time for both.

I was a single parent for summers and holidays and alone for the rest of the year. Both were hard and really gave me a clear perspective on this off the bench principle. Life is too short not to love what you are doing. When I left coaching and first moved to Corporate America, I had days when I wanted to walk away. Coaching had been fun. Basketball was fun. But in my new position, I wasn't having any fun.

A mentor and close friend encouraged me to take an account of all I had—people, possessions, spiritual foundation, and hobbies—and also to remind myself *why* I was doing what I was doing. What were the reasons to stay? He told me to compare this list to the list of reasons I was unhappy. His wisdom: "As long as the left side of your ledger is longer than the right, there is reason to be thankful." This simple act of remembering all the good in my life gave me a new perspective on where I was, and it gave me the courage to go after what I wanted with renewed passion and enthusiasm. It's a great life; sometimes, you just have to remind yourself.

Count Your Blessings

I recall a sales team that got off to a slow start; the leader was full of fire, but his team was mired in drama and unable to get any enthusiasm going. He asked me for help, so we created a message for him to send to each of their homes over Thanksgiving. He asked every person on the team to take a moment over the holiday to take a 360-degree view of their lives, noting all they had to be thankful for. He then asked them to look at where things stood at work and how they might improve things and add some business fun.

Just like when my mentor friend had me make my lists all those years ago, the act of listing out their blessings had a renewing effect on the team. They ran over their goal for the remainder of the year, coming close to being top in their division.

Schedule "Monday Nights"

Passion for work, working out, or even family is great and vital, but without balance, you will burn out.

A former boss and mentor, Tom Fioretti, gave me some advice I've never forgotten. He told me that as kids grow, your slice of their life will become smaller and smaller. You have to earn your slice daily. I took this to heart. Early on in my life as a single dad, my daughter Carly and I started having dedicated dad/daughter time. "Monday Night" was a meeting I did not miss. Whether doing an activity or just sitting together and catching up on life, it was sacred to us both. As time went on, the amount of our quality time together grew well beyond Monday nights.

As a single dad, I occasionally took Carly out in the field with me. She was always well behaved, and we both enjoyed the extra time together. Once, while I was a sales rep for Converse shoes, I had to bring her to a meeting with a store owner. I loaded her up with her dolls and toys and told her if I made a sale I'd buy her a prize. We couldn't leave her alone in the front of the store, so she came into his office and sat behind me, playing with her dolls while we met.

After my presentation, I began packing up. The owner was raving about how good Carly had been during the meeting when he looked at her and said, "What's wrong, little girl? You look sad." Not one to mince words, Carly said, "My dad said if you bought shoes today he would buy me a prize." We took dad/daughter time to a new level that day, tag teaming on a sale.

Balance it Out. Go Have Some Fun.

It was during those years with Carly that I learned the value of focusing on family. As our relationship grew, I saw the value of blending work and life. I still do a pretty good job of it today, but I'm not perfect. What is perfect is the relationship Carly and I have, and I credit those years of dedicated quality time. She has a life and family of her own today, but she still connects with me weekly. While it's no longer the official "Monday Night," it is quality time. These days we spend it virtually, using FaceTime or Skype to connect and talk about life. As much as I love my work, I love it more knowing it helped me give Carly a good start in life.

It isn't always feasible or even possible to go out and grab your dream job "right now." There's a lot of waiting on the road to true work fulfillment. Because of that, I just can't say this enough: find—and do—what makes you happy and surround yourself with people you love. Balance it out. I have two brothers I connect with often. Being with them reminds me how much I love the traditions and culture we grew up with and passed on to our own children.

I love fitness and challenging myself every day at the gym. Much like what I've done in my career, I love doing what I'm told someone my age shouldn't do. After an operation, I was told I'd never run again. I decided to rewrite that rulebook, and I can now run a 5K.

There's nothing like a good concert—seeing an artist doing what drives their passion—to get the blood flowing. I'll take in any kind of music, especially with a group of friends. I travel often for work, so instead of pining for home, I stop and smell the roses. It's a big, wonderful world filled with incredible people.

I live each day trying to be so good I can't be ignored. I live to be a positive influence and to make a difference, no matter how small. In short, I love what I do and I have fun—wherever I go.

Get in the Game

So how do you go about loving what you do, especially if things aren't perfect? Here are some things that work for me.

Long ago, I adopted something called the method of nine, and it's how I remember to check in with myself. It's pretty simple: spend nine minutes every day reminding yourself what gets you up in the morning. Spend fewer now and then if you must, but never more than nine minutes. Why nine? It's a pretty special number. To name a few examples, there are nine muses in Greek mythology, nine players on a baseball diamond, nine justices on the Supreme Court, and it takes nine months to bring a new baby into the world. Now you'll never forget: take nine minutes a day to consider what gets you out of bed and into the world.

As you catch yourself feeling happy or having a great time at work, make a mental note of it. What were you doing? How can you create more opportunities for that feeling?

Get involved in professional groups, clubs, or a stretch project. Being involved and around other people is a great way to find the fun.

It's a fact that people get more joy from giving than receiving. Be generous with sincere compliments. Extend kindness to people who are struggling. Be a mentor; help guide someone who needs direction. Bring in snacks for a meeting; it's amazing how a little food changes the mood of a room. Get involved with or start a company service project to help your community.

Survey your team and find out what they like to do for fun and how they like to be recognized. Run a fun contest. We ran a great contest in our Boston office called "Under Weight and Over Plan" emphasizing health and fitness and exceeding your goals.

Keep your family and loved ones at the top of your list, and give them the attention they deserve. Create a Monday Night type event and keep it sacred. You will never regret it.

It sounds simplistic, but smile. Even when it hurts. Others will smile back and bring a little happiness to even the toughest days.

COACH'S CORNER

- Find out what drives you, and follow the joy.

- Have a road map and use it. Take risks, and hang in there during the rough patches.

- When you're feeling low, count your blessings. Keep the "right side of the ledger longer than the left."

- Prioritize finding ways to make business fun, and prioritize family even above that.

- Do fun things.

ROADMAP
TO THE STARS

Chapter 8

BUILD A
GREAT TEAM

*Leaders must always be looking for and
developing great talent so that others are ready
to step in and make a difference when change
happens. Make it about the team from day one,
and be open to learning from them.*

Early on in my career as a women's basketball coach, a mentor shared with me a lesson I carry to this day. He said, "Speed and athleticism never take a vacation; when in doubt, take them to battle." I took that lesson to heart, and from then on, rule number one for my success was getting great talent.

Sometimes talent finds you. We received a letter and video at ODU from a girl from New York Mills, Minnesota, named Janet Karvonen. A high-scoring forward for her high school team, Janet had hopes to play Division I basketball and the initiative to reach out to us. I read her clips and viewed her tape; we were impressed. Coach Stanley sent me to Minnesota to see her in action.

Getting to New York Mills meant flying into Fargo, North Dakota, where winter can be brutal. I arrived and sure enough, it was cold. Really cold. It was the first time I had to plug a car in to keep the engine from freezing. Fortunately, Janet did not disappoint; she had an incredible night scoring. She wasn't overly quick, and at five-foot-ten she was short for a forward, but she had instinct, smarts, and a terrific work ethic. She would have to make a transition to small forward or guard to play at our level, but her talent and her fight were just what we were looking for. We recruited her, and she came to play at ODU.

It was great watching Janet's talent unfold; we were all proud of the player she became. Her natural talent was undeniable, and because of her work ethic, will to win, and competitive spirit, she had a great college career. I've got more stories like Janet's too; one of the highlights of my career was coaching someone up to their potential. There is no substitute for talent, and combined with hard work, the sky's the limit.

In my first year as a sales leader, I had a kid come in and interview. He was loosely dressed, not put together at all. This didn't exactly scream professionalism, and I typically would have cut the interview short and wished him well, but this kid had a spark. He'd grown up in East LA, a rough part of town, and he had a confidence that impressed me.

Point-blank, I asked him why I should hire someone who came to an interview dressed the way he had. He said, "Because I will be your best rep. And I'll run through a wall for you." I thought for a moment. Those are the raw qualities that make a great salesperson. I sent him home to put on a suit and tie and asked him to come back. He did, and sure enough, he became my best rep. Not only was he my best rep, but as his career continued, he became one of the best reps in the company. Today he's an executive for a large computer networking company. Again, raw talent, especially when accompanied by drive and determination, goes a long, long way.

Talent: the Constant Factor

Talent never takes a vacation. If you've got it, you've got it. So go get it. It worked on the court, and it works in the office. During my coaching career, teams I was associated with won nearly three hundred games and lost fewer than fifty. In the ten years I coached college hoops, we made it to nine post-season tournaments and three Final Fours. We won two national championships. We played twice in the women's version of the National Invitation Tournament, winning one championship. We had two Players of the Year and several All-Americans. I coached a total of seven future Olympians.

In business, I led teams for fifteen years. They made or exceeded plan fourteen times and made twelve President's Clubs—the equivalent to an NCAA top honor in that arena. The constant factor among all my teams? Talent.

In basketball, we recruited and developed great athletes: Nancy Lieberman, arguably the best to ever play the game, and two-time Olympic gold medalist Anne Donovan. To name a few more, Misty Thomas, Chris Critelli, and Inge Nissen all had the kind of big talent that made a coach's life easier. These top-level players attracted other players with exceptional natural ability. I saw the same thing in business, and in both arenas, they never came just to play; they came to compete…every day.

Don't kid yourself about your ability. Yes, the role of the leader is absolutely critical; but find an exceptional leader or coach, and I guarantee you'll find exceptional talent all around them. Without it, you can't win big. A great coach has great players, and a great leader has great people. Every time. Even in Cinderella stories during March Madness, you're looking at a team stacked with natural talent.

Be Overstaffed

Go into recruiting assuming you will lose people. Take the approach that you have to find and build talent constantly, because there's someone out there waiting to take your best and brightest away from you. Without the proper investment in them once you've got them, you will not be able to keep them. People are exposed to opportunities today both inside and outside their organizations with a few keystrokes or swipes of the finger. Talent will move up and move on. Plan to stockpile your organization with talent. Be overstaffed.

When leading off the bench, you are always looking for talent, always trying to find the next great superstar, always overstaffed. I develop leaders for a living. The common mistake both leaders and their leaders make when it comes to long-term sustainable success is a failure to be overstaffed with great talent. An Off the Bench Leader knows they have to pay attention to their pipeline on a regular basis.

With great talent, you can be great for a long time. In my role as a leadership development executive, I repeatedly observe that first-year leaders who are overstaffed by one or two people, and who take the time to develop and mold their entire teams, make their first goals. As a matter of fact, in one business unit I worked with, the average percentage of plan for the new leaders who were overstaffed by one or two was 108 percent.

Anticipate Success

I knew a very talented VP from Nashville. His people loved him; he had a fantastic career path, and he was game for bigger and better things. Sadly, his bosses did not nurture his growth and provide opportunities for him; he left for a bigger role in another company. That happens all the time, I know, but that's not the end of the story. What didn't need to happen was the gaping hole his departure left. Because they weren't invested in maximizing all their people and weren't anticipating success and recognizing there would be movement, there was no succession plan. They had no one ready to step in and take his place.

As an Off the Bench Leader, you put your team in a position to win, and one way to do that is to focus on bringing in talent regularly. Have a plan for the inevitable success of your talented team members. Back when I was a sales executive, a mentor told me to never stop interviewing. He knew that to find the next big superstar, you have to wade through hundreds of candidates. I set aside Thursday afternoons from three to six and did nothing but interview. Even with a fully staffed team, I tried to average two interviews a week.

When the Team Wins, Everyone Wins

If talent is number one, team unity is a close second. Time and time again, I've seen leaders underestimate the value of a tight team. When you look at great winning teams, unfailingly there is a bond among the members. They all get along, everyone accepts their role, and no one loses sight of the overall goal. They know that when the team wins, everyone wins.

A tight team will always share an identified common goal. The winning ODU teams, while being intensely competitive as individuals, all knew that the goal was one thing: a national championship. Consider this: Nancy Lieberman, the best player on those teams, willingly changed her role. She scored less and passed more, and she did it for the benefit of the team. In actuality, every person on that team made some sort of sacrifice; we had fifteen players, all capable of playing full time for other teams. Creating the kind of culture to attract and keep players of that caliber took the whole coaching team.

As coaches, one of our primary roles was keeping all that talent in check. Back when everyone called us "OD Who," we never had any doubt: they would beat the odds and win it all. Marianne Stanley developed that culture and set a high bar of success. We assembled all that talent and then gave them a strong buffet of skills and drills. This was a group that took extra shots after practice, came to practice early, and asked for coaching. In my first three years with this group, we lost only six games. We coached and developed their exceptional talent, taking them to higher levels than they dreamed were possible. That was Marianne's style; it was our style. It was always about the team.

Too many business leaders neglect to look at the whole team. Rather than manage and develop each member and create a culture of trust and oneness, they are content to ride with one or two superstars. As I think over all the sales teams I have had the opportunity to observe, I see the same makeup: clear goals, bold confidence born of talent, and a relentless pursuit of success. In particular, I see my first sales team, where eight of the nine members were brand new. They bonded early and often: through team meetings, friendly contests, after-work socials, monthly recognition dinners, and outings ranging from wine tastings to baseball games to bowling, a friendship and a strong sense of oneness formed. They shared an audacious goal, and everyone knew their role. As a result, they drove each other to success.

Great Teams Create Great Leaders

"You were my first sales coach! I was on the first team you managed. You really helped me develop my skills for bigger and better things."

—Carolyn Vineyard Schneider[1]

Your teams will remember how you treat them, what you say to them, and your particular nuances. They will all have stories to tell, so make sure they are telling the kind of stories you want repeated. Carolyn is one of the finest people I ever managed and a top salesperson to this day. She had the toughest assignment on the team, and she accepted it gladly. She loved feedback and coaching. We spent many hours together in the field, where I learned as much from her as she did from me. She had incredible perseverance and determination, and she never took no for an answer. Her will to succeed made me a better leader.

My first sales team taught me how to be transformational rather than transactional. Coaching basketball was a very directive skill. I blew whistles and barked orders. I directed the flow of every practice and urged my people on; it was very vocal. As a coach turned sales leader, this was something I needed to adjust. I came in like a basketball coach and nearly turned my team upside down. We got off to a poor start, and I was at fault.

A divisional vice president of sales knew I had the talent to lead, but saw I could use some guidance. He sent me to San Diego to take a Ken Blanchard course called Situational Leadership. That workshop changed my style and approach, and it laid the initial foundation for Off the Bench Leading. I was able to combine parts of my old style with my new learnings, and then the team did the rest, driving us to my first President's Club as a sales leader. The team got it done.

They were a young group; for many of them, it was their first job. But they were talented and because of that, they had no fear. On a mission to prove a point, they took on an "us against the world" mindset and ended up writing the guidebook for how to sell in an area where no one had any real success in the past. In fact, they crushed our goals. They became a band of brothers and sisters who came to work every day to compete and make the big plays. This was my ground-floor experience leading in Corporate America. This was where I first got off the bench.

Get in the Game

Building a talented team requires work. Thank goodness modern technology is here to help us find great people. Social media alone makes it easier than ever before to find talent. There is really no excuse for not having a full bench. Make sure you are devoting a chunk of your time to poring over the resources available to you. See who's out there, and invite them in.

At every stage of leadership, put a premium on staffing. Plan to always be plus one, and make sure that bench player is someone you can't live without. Never stop looking for talent. I know what you're thinking right now: budgets, budgets! Of course, that plays a part. But let me ask you, if you brought in the kind of talent your company couldn't live without, would they tell you to let them walk away? I hope not.

Interview weekly. Set an annual interview quota for yourself and then do it. Set a specific block of time aside every week to meet possible candidates. If you have a large candidate pool internally, identify who your next players will be and work collaboratively with that department to put a timeline in place for them to transition over to your team.

Put plans in place to make your bench players indispensable. Assign them a mentor, put a learning plan in place, and have an application plan where they are not just learning but doing. In sales, work on profiling, prospecting, and getting referrals. The fact that organizations are getting flatter with less hierarchy means everyone must pitch in; team selling is becoming the norm. Your team may look much like a basketball team with different positions and roles to play as the century moves on, rather than a whole team of forwards.

Off the Bench Leaders are always promoting their people and looking for successors; they know how important holding onto great talent is, both to them and their organization. As a coach, I wanted fifteen starters on my team. Look at a successful college basketball program and you'll see most often that every time someone graduates, someone equally talented steps in and fills their role. It should be that way on your team too. Everyone you have should be ready to jump into the game and make an impact at any time.

Plan for at least one-third of your group to move up, on, or out annually. In the best-case scenario people are promoted; others move on, and some just won't fit. Look at historical data and what the overall churn rates are, and adjust.

As a basketball coach we had depth charts for every player. As a leader you should have depth charts for every team member. I'm not talking about their HR files. Make your own chart for your own team, away from all the company noise around succession planning. HR is indispensable and great at what they do, but they don't know your team the way you do. Build it out, preferably electronically. Who will replace whom, and where will they come from? List it out and update it frequently.

Find out the key skills each team member needs to make them successful at their job. Determine if they are well versed or if they need help with each of those skills, and give them the right development opportunities to build their confidence along with their skill set.

COACH'S CORNER

- There is no substitute for talent. Be over-staffed with great talent.

- Your best people will be promoted or move on; prepare for that.

- Build a strong team relationship and bond over a shared, far-reaching goal.

- Great teams create great leaders.

Chapter 9

MASTER
THE DETAILS

*Fundamentals are the little essentials
you must do daily to succeed. Do the little
routines daily, and the big things will happen.*

When my daughter got married, getting to "I do" was a long time in the making. The amount of preparation my daughter, Carly, and son-in-law, Mike, put into the event to make sure it went off without a hitch was incredible, and it all came down to details. Choosing a venue, forming a guest list, decorating, selecting flowers, and all the activities before and after required scheduling, review, and execution. Mastering the details ahead of time made for a smooth, memorable wedding day.

To get to the point where you are ready to get married, both emotionally and from a party-planning perspective, there are a lot of details and fundamentals to cover. From dividing up tasks, to determining shared values and priorities, to coordinating napkin colors and centerpieces for the reception, it takes a lot of groundwork to be ready to say "I do."

The whole wedding planning process reminded me of a

principle I've lived by as both a basketball coach and a corporate leader: practice the fundamentals and remember the details. When I look back at my own marriage, I can see one of my biggest mistakes: I didn't focus on the little things that keep a marriage going. The small things matter, whether it's a little wedding detail or a trip to the grocery store. The way you handle the basics sows the seeds for success or failure. Success—extraordinary, championship-level success—lies in the details.

Practice, Practice, Practice

NBA Hall of Fame player "Pistol Pete" Maravich, a prolific ball passer, handler, and shooter, was asked what he did to get so good. He replied that one of the great keys to his success was repetition. By working on the particular areas of basketball—ball handling, shooting, passing, dribbling—over and over again, he could control the details. As he mastered the skills, he saw change take place in his overall game. Sustainable success comes from repetition. Drill a few key things daily, and make them a part of your culture.

No matter how talented your people are, you still need to develop their ability. Even Super Bowl winners show up for training camp. The New York Yankees, whether you like them or not, have a storied championship record. They go out and get the best talent, and then that talent goes to practice. The UConn Huskies women's basketball team is another example; they practice, practice, practice, constantly honing their talent. There is no way anyone can sustain the long-term success they have without getting great talent and mastering the fundamentals daily. Watch them play, and it's apparent. The coaches put a premium on constant daily repetition of fundamentals, which makes players better year in and year out.

My first high school All-American, Cathy Rousseau, recalled how tough I was on the fundamentals. But she also recalled how it paid off: Catholic Central High School's girls' basketball team had a 55-2 record.

At ODU, we had station drills for every member of the team. Ranging from making simple layups to honing their rebounding skills, the coaches worked one on one with the players prior to and after regular team practice on these specific skills. For example, Angela Cotman, a small star guard who could jump out of a building from a standstill, had trouble with her pivot foot. We used a bell to help remind her to keep it still. Eventually, the skill became second nature to her. Nancy Lieberman, who I believe to be the best all-around player of all time, regularly stayed after practice and took shots and worked on her game. Despite her phenomenal natural ability, she knew she could always improve some part of her game. She was willing to do what others would not; that's what great champions do.

Nothing reminds me more of this than the first University of Hawaii team I coached. The coaching staff had small things for every member of the team to work on, drilling until they could execute at a championship level. Every player, from new to tenured, from the least skilled to the most gifted, worked relentlessly on passing, catching, rebounding, hustling on defense, making layups, shooting free throws, pivoting, and taking charges.

It had been many years since they'd had a winning season, but after a year of drilling fundamentals and daily mastering of details, the University of Hawaii team played their way to the program's first ever post-season tournament. They didn't have the depth of talent the teams from ODU had, but they had heart and a willingness to work at the little things—and perform them at a championship level.

You Have to Invest

I owe a great deal of my success to Dave Cannici, a VP of sales learning for a Fortune 500 company in New Jersey. He developed, supported, and created the initial opportunity for me to develop leaders, and it was through that relationship that I was able to find a stage to take my development to another level. Dave is passionate about development and mastering the details.

His model for looking at success—and failure—in sales is something I refer to often.

"To talk about failure in the upbeat, positive environment that exists in the typical sales culture is usually seen as taboo, but there are important lessons to be learned from looking at why there is always a contingent of sales associates who fail," he says. "Who truly owns the responsibility? We can debate this in general terms all day, but if you isolate what I believe the four main factors are, the picture suddenly becomes quite clear."[2] Dave uses a square, divided into four quadrants, to illustrate his point.

The four quadrants are filled with the terms *skill*, *capacity*, *value*, and *effort*. Were they thoroughly trained and given an opportunity to acquire the skills they needed? Were they hired appropriately? That is, do they have the capacity to understand and implement what makes a great salesperson? Did they see the value in what they were doing? Did the manager bring them along or "simply bark orders and inspect activity standards"?3 At the end of the day, only the fourth quadrant, effort, is the responsibility of the salesperson. Your people have to care, and they have to try. Beyond that, the responsibility for their success or failure rests largely with you, the manager. You have to invest in their development, especially in the area of skill.

Skill is generally defined as the acquired ability to do something well. Dave says the first reason sales associates fail is a lack of skill, which is not to be confused with talent or ability. When an associate with the requisite drive, attitude, and opportunity lacks the skill set necessary to do their job well, that is a reflection not on them, but on the manager who failed to coach, model for, and teach them what they needed to know. Every team meeting I led had a learning/training portion to it. I called on the people who currently modeled the skills the best and had them demonstrate and deliver to the rest of the team. After everyone knew what we were shooting for, I sent them away to practice and practice some more—until it was second nature for everyone.

OMG! (And It's Not Oh My Gosh)

When I say OMG, it stands for observe, monitor, and give. The only way you can do that is to be off the bench and around your people. First, find out what your people need through observation. Next, coach them through repetition, role-play, and recognition to get those new skills to stick. Then, give the right feedback at the right time. Sounds easy, right? Yet it's rarely done. Ask most leaders if they have profiled their team to determine what they need coaching on, and you'll get a few yeses. Ask for evidence of their coaching and follow-through, and you're not likely to find it.

Championship level leading means never letting the fundamentals go untouched. Identify the fundamental skills you want to see, and then watch your people. Ken Blanchard's Situational Leadership model stipulates that people go through a development process for each task or goal they want to master. At any given time, they are either learning or performing. If they are learning, they need direction. If they are performing, they need support.

If it's important enough for you to give feedback around, then it's even more important to recognize them for doing it right. I asked the same two questions at every emerging leader class for six years. First, "Who here has recently received feedback from their leader?" Nine of ten hands went up. Then I asked, "Who here received recognition for or review of that feedback at a later date?" Eight of the nine hands went down. OMG. Something important is missing.

Do yourself and any team you have the opportunity to lead a big favor. OMG all the time. Make it truly about them by recognizing the good behaviors and coaching through those that need improvement. I knew of a sales leader who held one of his team members back from learning because he didn't want them out of the office for training. He was concerned this employee's absence would negatively affect *him.* Needless to say, that sales person is now on another team, thriving at a high level. His new leader observed his desire for development and aligned with him, giving him the opportunities and support he needed to excel.

Great leaders seem to live to develop and teach people to be better. Marianne Stanley, head coach at ODU during the great years and now with the WNBA, epitomized this. She never let a good move go unrecognized, and she pointed out every key skill that needed improvement. Marianne never let up on the basics: boxing out, pivoting, catching, bounce passing, etc., and as a result, everyone got better. It was her constant observation and monitoring, resulting in the most useful feedback, that led to a mastery of the details and made a talented team extraordinary.

Practice? When?

The twist is this: In business, when, exactly, do you have time to practice? You play the game all day, every day, then spend time with family at night and have the weekend for hobbies and chores. The best leaders I have observed in my corporate experience *find* the time; they are always training their teams to be better. They understand you can't *do* what you don't know *how* to do, so they make learning a priority. There is never a perfect time to practice, but the best leaders find ways to fit it in. They target skills and tasks for each person on their team, then identify areas for improvement and drill down on them, training, giving feedback, and leveraging big data for reinforcement.

Get in the Game

Throughout my leadership career, I've emphasized mastery of the fundamentals. These are the little essentials you have to do daily to succeed. Basketball teams are required to do the same things over and over: pass, dribble, catch, hustle, box out, make free throws, and make layups. In sales, it's things like prospecting, hitting appointment goals, and being prepared, knowledgeable, and bold on a call. These are the things that, with practice and repetition, every team can perform to 100 percent. They are the groundwork for team chemistry and rhythm.

As a leader, you have your own fundamentals to drill. Your ability to run a one on one, a team meeting, or a field/seat ride sets the tone for your whole team. So do your willingness to listen, your delivery of constructive feedback, and your situational coaching and leading. And don't underestimate the impact your conversations and messaging have on your success. Give yourself time to reflect on your interactions at the end of each day. Consider the conversations that went well and those that could have gone better. Use this information to practice and perfect your communication. Spend time focusing on both tactical and fire-mode skills. The tactical leads to day-to-day success, making the fire skills less frequently necessary.

Observe your people regularly. The best way to do that? Roll up your sleeves. Get in there with them, off the bench. You will learn most of what you need to know from this alone. The best sales leaders spend the bulk of their time in selling activities, coaching, and sales innovation.

Determine the keys to extraordinary success for your team. Make a list, survey the group, and study the data. Within each skill, assess each person. Ask yourself, "Where is this person with this skill? Are they new, learning to be good, good, or a champion?" Then, align with them by asking them where they think they stand and how they will get to the championship level. Put in place a development plan both for individuals and team-wide.

Now, monitor and guide them. Give appropriate feedback, recognition, and coaching. Do this daily, even with your best people. Low support is infinitely more valuable than no support.

Try a round robin approach to team learning. The key to this is quick, impactful learning. Identify key behaviors and skills your people need to master, then find experts among the ranks. Set up a room with stations, each with a topic and an expert to deliver high-impact learning with an accompanying action. Run the stations, depending on the number of topics, anywhere from twenty to forty minutes, and give only a few minutes to get to the next station.

Our video-clip-watching, sound-bite-consuming culture supports a fast, action-based approach to learning; your team will enjoy this, and they will learn a lot. Try these stations to work through any skill—from gaining access to handling objections—in a fun, highly interactive environment. Over time, repetition will imbed the skill. Follow up a round robin station session at your next meeting. Have people share what they implemented in the field and the results.

Expect your people to take ownership of their skills, and never stop refining your own. Even though I no longer lead a team, I spend time every morning sharpening my skills. From keeping up with technology, to practicing all forms of communication, to keeping forward on the hottest trends in leadership, commit to being a lifelong learner. It's fundamental.

COACH'S CORNER

- Know what fundamentals are key to your and your team's success and which ones need work.

- Practice and repeat. Repetition leads to belief; once belief sinks in, miracles begin to happen.

- Invest in your team. Hire well, develop their skills, and bring them into the vision with you.

- OMG: profile your people, then give the right feedback and coaching at the right time.

- Establish a culture of learning with regular interactive skill-development sessions. Keep learning yourself too.

Chapter 10

MARK
YOUR PROGRESS

*Aim high and plan thoroughly. Nothing beats looking
back at what you were able to endure or overcome to
reach a goal. Each obstacle builds the bridge to success.*

Down by one point with two minutes to go in a post-season game, Hawaii had the ball and a three-on-two breakaway advantage. It could have been our moment, but our point guard decided to pull up at the top of the key and launch a jumper that went off the rim. Opportunity lost, game over, and the first post-season game ever for this program went into the record books. In the heat of the moment, I felt it was a selfish shot to take and pulled the guard out of the game. All I could see was that game; I was frozen in that moment.

As we sat there watching the game clock run out, my assistant reminded me of all the hurdles we'd overcome just to get to that point. She was right; I decided that instead of focusing on this loss, I would remind everyone of the many positive steps we'd taken to get there. We'd crossed so many bridges. The season prior, that same team won less than ten games, yet here they were in post-season play. The biggest breakthrough came after the first road trip, when we lost our first three games. The kids really responded to the challenge of taking it to another level, and practices became more robust and intense after that. Like laying bricks one at a time, each game, each individual win along the way accumulated and built a path to an extremely successful season.

Mapping It Out

During my first coaching job at Catholic Central High School, I spent hours at the kitchen table of my mentor, Don Bassett, now a Hall of Fame coach at Catholic Central. Don took an early interest in me and was very influential in my development. The most valuable lesson I learned from him concerned planning and marking your progress. Coach Bassett mapped out his entire season game by game, and it was easy to see this was a huge key to his success. He knew to a degree where his team should be at any given point in the season. Don had the Xs and Os down to a science, and he spent many hours teaching me how to see the game.

We took strategic planning to a whole new level at ODU; Marianne Stanley and I sat many long, pre-season days and nights planning practices, diagraming plays, and outlining strategies for the upcoming season. We tested each defense strategy with a chess-like game of nickels and dimes to see how they played out. We would go back and forth, testing plays and defense. "What if they did this?" and "What if we did that?" On and on.

We carried the deliberate planning over to practice, where sometimes we charted shots and rebounds as a way of understanding just where everyone was and what trends we might find on shot selection and percentage. Marianne, another Hall of Fame coach, was a very strategic thinker on the court; in my opinion, one of the best of all time. She brought that into games and as a result, she knew where the team was at any given minute. I love knowing the many hours we spent planning during those early days at ODU were bricks in the path to her extraordinary success.

Straight out, every role I've ever had required hours and hours of planning. Fortunately for me, I've always been a planner so I adapted easily. In my earliest days, I even drew plans for basketball practice on my lunch bag. With all the technology we have today, the lunch bag and the multiple hours are no longer necessary, but a solid plan is still indispensable. Consider this: at CCHS, the teams I coached lost only three games in four years; at ODU, Marianne and I led our teams to victory in all but six games in our first three years; and as a sales leader I missed plan only once in fifteen years. I'd call that solid evidence in the case for having a plan.

Celebrate the Small Stuff

In any organization, a leader aspiring to greatness will leverage every victory. From day one, take every win, no matter how small, and shout it to the moon. Recognize the behaviors you want to see, then give feedback and recognition. Creating a climate where every success merits a celebration will drive the culture.

By leveraging a lot of small bridges rather than relying solely on one huge one, you'll get a lot more people across the river. When learning how to cook, you don't start with a full-blown, gourmet meal for twelve. You go one recipe at time, making a list, shopping for groceries, prepping and timing it out. It's the same thing in business leadership. Break your goals down into steps, and as you complete each one, take a minute and celebrate.

Chart Your Journey

I'd be lying if I said I wasn't proud of the awards and honors I've won over the years, but what I truly relish are the memories I made along the way. My first high school team, the girls at CCHS, were so inspiring with their work ethic. The first win at ODU was a feeling I'll never forget. It was truly remarkable coaching world-class athletes. Making President's Club, especially the first time, was a thrill. I also remember vividly the first time I missed President's Club. Not my best day. And I remember a heartbreaking loss for ODU in the National Tournament, a loss that cost us a third national title.

Those memories from the past, both good and bad, are responsible for the insights I'm able to share today. It is important to not just have a plan, but also to mark your progress. In sales, it is easy. There's always a board to measure your progress against your goal, but go beyond that. We have endless data at our fingertips today; seeing where you are and why you are there is easier than ever before.

Marking your progress helps you stay—or get back—on track and overcome unforeseen challenges that become detours on the way to success. Wouldn't it be nice to have a highway to success? I'd love four lanes. The reality is, the economy can change with the wind. Having an adaptable plan and data at your fingertips gets the group around those detours sooner. As the leader, it's your job to stay the course, or occasionally chart a new one.

Even the Best-Laid Plans

Inevitably, there will be times when things get off course. April Jacob, a VP of sales for a Fortune 500 company in Houston, Texas, knows this all too well. April had experienced nothing but success in her career—until one of the largest hurricanes ever to hit the Gulf Coast turned all her plans upside down. She was one month away from maternity leave when the hurricane struck, and when she came back, she returned to a devastated team.

"They were not making sales," she shares. "Many could not even enter their territories, thus they were not making money. I came back to a team that was a shell of its former glory and positivity. They were 20 percent behind the sales goal for the year, negative, and frustrated."[1] April didn't expect to recover before the end of the fiscal year, so she set out to finish the year not driving toward a financial goal, but by demonstrating calm under pressure and developing team unity and camaraderie.

April got off the bench, way off, and began to work side by side with her team. "I held team events despite being repeatedly under plan; we celebrated birthdays and small wins; I sent letters home to their spouses and significant others. I wanted them to know that we won and lost *together*." It worked; the whole team stayed together despite the incredible adversity they faced.

Imagine their delight when the books closed on the year. After not making a commission check for five months, April was ready for a fresh start. Everyone was. The market recovered, and the team went on to have their best year ever. April's willingness and ability to adjust the team's plan to the situation saved the team and formed a bond that stands to this day among its members, despite everyone having moved on in their careers.

It's All Good. As Long As You Learn Something.

Losses are inevitable; no one goes undefeated. Resilience is another key marker of an Off the Bench Leader. It's understanding what went wrong and putting a plan in place to fix it. It's the first practice after a tough game; you watch the film as a team, identifying your mistakes. It's the first month or quarter you miss your business goals, reviewing the data objectively and putting an adjusted plan in place.

Even when your plans need changing or don't turn out at all, the time you spent planning will have been worth it. Mistakes in planning lead you to something absolutely critical: the knowledge and experience you gain. The team grows closer through adversity, and learning from a tough time is almost always followed by a run of success. At the close of the season, ask any sports team, from the World Champions to the last in the league, what their year was like. Inevitably, they will tell you what they learned and how they are positioning themselves for what's to come.

Get in the Game

This is one area where leading a business team is not much different than coaching a sports team. Through step-by-step planning, you can lay out your entire year, player by player, and easily understand where your business is coming from:

- *Daily:* find time to sit and identify the biggest return on your time. Are there high-value decisions that need to be made?

- *Nightly:* capture the highlights of the day, then plan your next.

- *Monthly:* Big plans take time; carve out a date with yourself to focus on projects, people, and processes. Assess where you are; what do you need to do to reach your goal? Consider which relationships you should nurture and which ones might be taking you away from your target.

- *Annually:* Take some time to reset yourself. You can identify many different reset buttons within a year: January 1, a fiscal marker, a new season, and more. Personally, I like to use my birthday. This is an opportunity to really mark your milestones and get intentional about getting where you want to go.

Distractions will happen, so put a velvet rope around your plan. Choose what's worth your time and what you must pay attention to. As someone told me, "Be the bouncer of an exclusive club." Keep out anyone who wants to take you away from your VIP items, aka your plan0As a matter of fact, over a five-year span in one business unit, the new sales executives running through the SCADD model collectively averaged 108 percent of their goal vs. 98 percent for those who did not. Here's a breakdown of SCADD. Some of this will be familiar from other chapters:

- *S: Staffing.* That's job number one. Find talent and never stop looking. Set time aside weekly to recruit and interview candidates. Set an annual goal of how many people you would like to interview in a fiscal year. It will take a lot of looking to find that one superstar you cannot live without.

- *C: Challenge and Channel Effectiveness.* Challenge your people on who they meet with regularly. Know who they are meeting with and challenge them by questioning, "Are these people decision makers who can help you advance?" Channel Effectiveness is about your people developing both internal and external partners and determining if they are getting referrals or testimonials from those partners.

- *A: Activity Advancement.* Know what drives your business. Understand the levers that move the business, and rank your people against these levers. Ensure your people understand the metrics. Review the messaging around each lever; work this into your daily routine. People who know where to focus and what to say will have an easier time advancing activity.

- *D: Development.* Have a development plan based on the metrics above for each person on your team. Knowledge of their job and how they message that to others is the key to success. Whether it's sales or something else, getting your people from good to great around the key tasks will help your team build skill and confidence.

- *D: Days Between or Without Events.* Know how many days people go without key activity, and understand the reasons. Prioritize moving people to shorter time spans between events by understanding what's happening and how you can overcome that. Holding your people to specified outcomes will catapult your business and help them grow as well.

To get a struggling team on track, focus on trust, reset commitments and expectations, and keep your eye on results. Minimize conflicts and if necessary, deliver a new plan. The more you plan ahead and prepare for varying outcomes, the sooner you can get the team back on track.

Hold your team accountable to results. Check in regularly on their progress, and celebrate all victories.

COACH'S CORNER

- Plan to succeed.

- Identify and celebrate small wins along the way.

- Chart your journey. Check in regularly and adjust where you need to.

- Things change, sometimes for the worse. Focus on team and trust to get through a rough patch.

- Learn from everything.

Chapter 11

HAVE COURAGE

During your lifetime you will be presented with countless opportunities. If you possess the courage to grasp a few of them, they will change your life. You can't taste victory without risking defeat.

Growing up, Mom and Dad had their rules, but we walked to school on our own, went out and played sports on our own, and wreaked our fair share of havoc in the house when they went out for the night and left us home alone. Ultimately, they trusted our judgment, confident we'd make the right decisions. When we got out of line, they simply put us back on the path.

I cherish memories of days off school playing football in the fresh winter snow and ice skating down the frozen river. Dad probably wouldn't have been too thrilled about the ice skating, but those are the kinds of risks you take as a free and fearless kid—both the skating and the possibility of getting caught. Mom always had hot cocoa and fresh Italian cookies made from scratch; maybe that's part of why I remember it so fondly as well.

In large part, courage stems from the opportunities you were given as a child to take risks, make mistakes, and survive to take on another day. It's the opportunities you create for others to take the same risks and be brave and bold about chasing a dream or purpose worth accomplishing. I often hope I gave my daughter, Carly, the same freedom to create her own memories and build her own confidence. I know I tried my best. You may not think of yourself as particularly courageous or remember any great acts of daring from your childhood, but I've got news for you. If you're aspiring to any sort of leadership, you are brave. Believe it.

Take the First Leap

A swim coach said to me once, "I want everyone in the water swimming as fast as they can and to the best of their ability, but I also want them to do it in the deep end." I love that. Do your best, but always make sure there's a risk attached. That's how we achieve dreams. The hardest moves and toughest decisions you make, the ones that require the most courage, may take years to reveal their full value. Choosing to leave the championship basketball program at ODU for an unknown, unproven program at University of Hawaii was a huge risk. Some of the rewards were apparent within a few years, as I saw the program grow in success, reputation, and confidence, but I could never have anticipated the way things would unfold years later.

Leaving coaching, my first love, for a business I knew nothing about was a crazy risk, but it has paid off every year of my life since then. In one of my favorite examples, and one that brings us full circle to my choice to lead the University of Hawaii team, years after I'd joined ADP, the company was opening an office in Hawaii. Someone remembered I'd lived and coached there many years prior. This led to an opportunity, which in turn led to a big promotion when I was chosen to open and lead that new office. Had I not taken that first leap of faith, the second would never have been possible.

At another major career intersection, I left the comfort of a job in Southern California, where I led a highly successful team, for a position in Florida across the country and out of my comfort zone. Once again it was an enormous risk, but it paid off in countless ways. The previously struggling team became wildly successful, but perhaps even more important was the leadership lesson I learned about moving people boldly toward a common goal, a foundation of Off the Bench Leading.

Just Stretch

No barrier was ever broken without courage. From the first flight, to the first moon landing, to ordinary people who strapped into a paraglider or cliff jumped for the first time, their actions took guts. Here's some good news for you. You don't need to do anything like that to be bold or brave. You just need to size up your environment and take calculated risks that stretch you, or your team, a little bit more than you would like.

Courage takes on many faces in leading today. It's holding firm on ethics regardless of implied threats, and it's taking the mission, vision, and strategy and changing it midstream to get a team back on track or elevate performance. It takes a lot of courage to stand up and make the change, and even more to stay the course and make it stick.

I don't have any grandiose tales of courage, but I can tell you

I got up after every setback in my life, recovered after every loss, and fought back and reinvented myself over and over again. I was a good athlete, not a great one; a good coach, not a great one; and I was a good leader. Combined, this gave me the courage to tackle developing leaders and getting up in front of audiences and speaking to rooms filled with smart, savvy, successful people. It was a long process to get from where I started—a nervous, dry-mouthed, constantly pacing speaker—to where I am now— continually humbled by positive reviews.

Act As If

No one would look at me, much less talk to me. I stood there at my first regional sales meeting, a newly appointed sales executive and waited for someone to at least say hello. I had earned the role through my performance elsewhere, where I'd proven myself as a leader in just eighteen months, but no one here knew that or cared. I'd have thought my background as a championship basketball coach would spark a little curiosity or invite conversation, but it clearly did not. People walked by me like I wasn't even there. What was I doing there? In that moment, I wanted nothing more than to go back to my old office.

What *was* I doing there? I'd gotten the job over the most popular sales person in the office. Many had assumed his promotion was a given, so my arrival was a bit of a shock. True, the VP who hired me and I had a connection from being born and raised in the same part of upstate New York. We even knew some of the same people, though we'd never met. But this guy was sharp— much too sharp to hire someone based on a former shared zip code. He'd had another reason.

The salesman who didn't get the job was a great guy, and he had great numbers. It wasn't anything he did that lost him the role; in fact, he didn't lose it at all. Rather, I won it. And I won it by acting "as if." Early on, I put a stake in the ground and told the world, or at least the company, that I was their next leader. As I said, this guy was very good. He was excellent, in fact, and he went on to a long and successful management career enjoying the respect of many, including me. But for that one role, I had acted as if I were already in the role just a little bit more. Sometimes, that's all the edge you need.

Flash back to me, standing there wondering what I could do to break the ice with everyone. A funny thing happened: one of my new sales people came up to me and said, "You look nervous."

I said, "I am! I'm not sure if I will fit in by the reaction I'm getting."

She replied, "Don't worry. Act as if you've been here all along. You'll be fine."

And that's exactly what I did. It's how I'd gotten the job, after all. From my first day with the company, I'd been acting as if this promotion were inevitable. I brought that confidence into the meeting; my team and I connected, and thus began a run of terrific sales success.

If You Wait for Perfect Conditions, You'll Never Get Anything Done

February 17, 2013, is a day I'll never forget. Old Dominion University was honoring alumni, and it was the first time I'd been invited back. I hadn't seen the Lady Monarchs play at home in thirty years. I was treated like royalty by players, coaches, alumni, and fans. They won a nail biter in the final seconds, and during halftime many esteemed alumni were honored for their contributions. These were memory-making moments, but what stands out for me is the name Sara Jones.

Sara was an assistant coach for the team, and she'd lost a brave battle with cancer just two days earlier. What inspired me that afternoon and will forever leave a mark was the character, poise, and cadence the Lady Monarchs showed. Just two days earlier these women had lost one of their coaches, yet they went out and played through the pain. The conditions for play were far from perfect. They easily could have folded; it would have been entirely understandable, but they went out and executed, even in unimaginably tough conditions.

Their poise and determination got me thinking. How often in Corporate America do sales teams face tough days, tough odds, and tough conditions? Although the loss of a leader is a rare and extreme example, every day on every team there is someone who is facing a challenge. From illness to injury to personal crises, we've all got our hurdles to cross. As a leader, are you in possession of the confidence and courage to rally those people? This I've come to know: there is no such thing as perfect conditions. Just when you think you're close, something brings you back to earth.

You never know when that tough day is coming; but your everyday actions will guide your team and give them the courage they need to face it when it does. Clearly, Coach Sara had lived the kind of life and fought the kind of battle that inspired her players to go out and win, even in the wake of grief and pain. I'll never forget February 17, 2013, or what it taught me about real courage.

Step Up, or Step Back?

Ken Polk, a leadership development executive for a Fortune 500 company in Buffalo, New York, shared a story that really hit home on the subject of courage. He told of a manager who had just made his company's President's Club for the third straight year. In fifteen years, he'd never made so much money. To the outside world, he was basking in success, and to a degree, he was. There were parts of the job he enjoyed, but there were also many things that frustrated him.

Then someone asked him a question. "Are you happy?" With those three words, he realized how much he missed being in the field, selling. He was a good manager, but he was a great salesperson. Faced with this information, he made the courageous decision to leave management and return to direct sales, where he enjoyed a successful—and happy—career. Ken said, "Sometimes people find that even though they want to be managers, they truly are better off in other positions; it takes courage to admit that and move into another role."[1] Sometimes, it's not about stepping up; sometimes, you're meant to step back.

To do this with confidence, identify—then lean upon—your support group. I was taught to look at my world as a diamond. If I'm in the middle, each facet represents a person I can go to for advice, mentoring, or support. Seeing yourself surrounded with facets of support makes risks much easier to take.

Meant to Shine

I love this quote from Marianne Williamson: "Our deepest fear is not that we are inadequate. Our deepest fear is that we are powerful beyond measure. It is our light, not our darkness that most frightens us … We are all meant to shine."[2]

We *are* all meant to shine, and at the end of the day, what that mostly requires of us is courage. To embrace the new and find out just how much we are capable of, we first have to release what is comfortable and seemingly secure. I've got news for you: there is no real security in what is no longer meaningful. Once you've lost your drive, you're just going through the motions, living on autopilot. Eventually, no matter how competent you are, that lack of passion will affect you and everyone around you. Therefore, your real security lies in the adventure and excitement of starting new journeys, of forging new paths. What path are you wanting to travel? And what are you waiting for? Grab your light. Start moving.

Get in the Game

As an Off the Bench Leader, you have to be bold. There are no magic steps involved in having courage. Just go with your gut and take calculated risks when they're worth the potential outcome.

Lay down the road map you want to follow and take small, incremental steps to get there. Once you can visualize your journey, confidence will come, fear will subside, and calculated, bold actions will be a natural part of your routine.

Conduct yourself as if you are interviewing for the role you ultimately want long before the job is posted. Emulate successful role models, take the advice of mentors, and seize opportunities to take practice shots whenever possible. This is a balancing act, and it requires an extra investment of time and effort up front. The key is to maintain your current level of performance while taking on stretch assignments to give you the exposure and experience necessary to elevate yourself to the next role.

Off the Bench Leaders act as if they are already in the next role. They are not worried about titles; they let their actions and results lay the groundwork. They take on the persona of the role they want. When your desired position comes available, and it will, there should be no question as to who the best candidate is. It will be you, hands down.

Things happen fast; your whole world could change tomorrow. Become the kind of person who anticipates and welcomes the choices, risks, and opportunities that are inevitably coming your way. How? In any situation where you could use a shot in the arm, just ask yourself this: What could happen? Write it down and play out a best- and a worst-case scenario. Use all the data at your disposal, and rely on your network to give you relevant, unbiased advice.

A courageous leader creates an environment where team members are not afraid to take risks; your courage drives their fear away. Developing people who feel safe enough to take chances is a hallmark of a successful Off the Bench Leader. Give them opportunities for risk—small and relatively safe at first, then bigger and bigger as they prove themselves.

Coach's Corner

- Take risks. One step at a time is just fine.

- Act as if you've already gotten the role you aspire to.

- Don't wait for things to be perfect. They never will be.

- Embrace your own talent. Believe you were meant to shine.

- Know when to step up, and recognize when to step back.

Chapter 12

SAY THANK YOU

Remember to thank the people you rely on to get the work done. Everyone counts and contributes every day. Let them know how much you appreciate their efforts.

Imagine a group of people, from an unsung team, that worked countless hours to bring value to their company. They worked diligently, often getting more done in a week than most teams do in two. Their results were noticed, and the boss they loved working for, who effectively motivated them to happily go that extra mile, was promoted. This supervisor always had time for them, even though she was pressed for time herself. She never forgot to say "nice job" and "thank you," even if it was a two-word text message. But now, this supervisor was gone.

Enter the new leader. Most everyone sent a welcoming, congratulatory note. After all, a big promotion is definitely worthy of recognition. Instead of acknowledging everyone who congratulated the leader, he chose to reply only to a select few. This sent a message from the beginning that not everyone was valued equally, and word got around. As time went on, very few people got recognition, creating an environment of competition and distrust where unity had once flourished. Not surprisingly, in six months' time people began leaving the team at every opportunity.

Life Is a Team Experience

Imagine going through your entire life without saying "thank you." Imagine being so self-absorbed that you end up ignoring everyone around you and being unaware of how they contribute to your success. Imagine running an organization in total isolation, never leaving your office to connect with anyone or give them a well-deserved pat on the back.

It's unimaginable, isn't it? We've all recognized the help and generosity of others at least a few times in our lives. As a leader, the occasional plate of cookies in the break room or "good job" email just isn't enough. You must recognize the contributions of others so often, it becomes part of your identity. Your team needs to know, without a doubt, that you recognize their value.

Elitist leaders concerned only with their own success sometimes make it, but they are missing out on the best part of leading: the relationships. All of life is a team experience. Everyone who touches you counts; all your interactions contribute to making you the best leader you can be. Consider this: in your lifetime, have you ever heard of anyone asking their boss, supervisor, leader, or coach to stop giving them recognition? I'm guessing not, but if you do know someone, please introduce me; I want to work for their boss.

Gratitude Is Free

I have a question for you. How difficult, really, is it to say "thank you," or "nice job"? With all the technology at our fingertips, getting a good word out is simple, yet sadly, it's not a common practice. I see it far too often, and it continually amazes me. You can train and develop people all you want, but without recognition, little becomes cultural. When you are growing a team, why would you not take a few minutes each day to acknowledge the people who put themselves out there for you? It costs you nothing to give someone a good word, but when recognition becomes part of your culture, the payoff—for everyone—is continual.

A fantastic model of this off-the-bench tactic is Carlos Rodriguez, the current CEO of ADP. Carlos is approachable, consistently gives feedback, and has a good word for everyone he comes in contact with. After delivering a training at an ADP office in New Jersey, I was putting my things away and cleaning up the room when, to my surprise, Carlos popped his head in and asked how it went. I said it had gone well, to which he replied, "You know, I hear good things about you."

I was both floored and elated, and I would have been completely satisfied with our encounter, but it didn't end there. He asked how I was getting back to my hotel. As everyone with a car had already left, I told him I planned to take a taxi. He said, "Give me a minute, I'll drive you." This is the CEO of a Fortune 500 company; the word *busy* barely scratches the surface of the demands on his time, yet he took the time to drive me back to my hotel. On that drive, you can believe I soaked up every word he said to me. And can you guess which ones meant the most? Yep, it was "Thanks for the great work." Taking a note from that encounter and how it made me feel, I have made it my mission to sincerely say to people, "Thanks for the great work," whenever it applies.

Being able to spot people doing things right and articulating your observation is a skill every leader needs in their toolbox. The praise reinforces the behavior and motivates them to repeat it again and again. No matter how far along you get in your career, this holds true. Just like anyone else, I enjoy specific, sincere, positive feedback. After a recent leadership class, one of my bosses commented on the way I quickly connect and establish relationships with my audience, putting everyone at ease. He could have just said "Nice opening," but by going a step further and telling me specifically what he liked, he anchored that behavior in my mind. You can bet I will now reinforce it every time I step in front of a crowd. It cost him nothing to say that to me, but it'll pay the company back for a long time by making me a better presenter.

You Have to Mean It

The key to delivering thanks and recognition is to mean it. When anyone says "Nice job" to me and I know there is sincerity behind it, it makes my day. Especially on a tough day, I find myself walking a little lighter. If I had to identify the single most key component of Off the Bench Leading, I would have to say it fits right here. You own you. You choose how to treat others. My question is this: Why would you choose to interact other than with integrity and sincerity?

The goal of any team is to accomplish a task, whether a single victory, a championship, a month on plan, or gaining the annual top honor in your company. The best way to do that—any of it—is for everyone to believe the work is worth doing; you need a shared purpose. As the leader, your honest appreciation for what each person brings to the table is a huge determinant of their buy-in. If you don't mean it, why should they?

If you don't thank your people, if they don't know without a doubt that you appreciate them, someone else will. I knew a stellar sales rep who wanted to pursue leadership. She did all the right things and came through her company's leadership development program with flying colors. When a position became available, she was hesitant to apply. Although her direct supervisor had put her in the program, their day-to-day interactions led her to believe he had no intention of supporting her. She felt any recognition she got from him was perfunctory at best, and frankly she didn't see the point in trying to advance. Today, she is a high-flying leader for another business within the same company, consistently moving up the ladder. Like I said, if you don't sincerely value your team members, the best of them will always find someone who will.

Raise the Stakes

A sincere and substantial recognition program can go a long way toward building drive and enthusiasm. I ran many during my years as a leader; two stand out in my mind for the huge dividends they brought in. Sure, we had to spend a little money, but I'm telling you, we came out ahead. First, we had the High Producers Club. This group, identified by indisputable data, sat at a special table at the quarterly group meeting, which was decorated to resemble a high-end restaurant. Their table was set beautifully and covered in linen, and throughout the meeting, they were catered to by a waitstaff. No box lunch buffet line for these superstars.

I also ran a wine club for the highest producers: team members who reached a specified level of performance received an engraved bottle of fine wine. The contents were enjoyed, and the bottles became keepsake reminders of a job not just well done, but gratefully recognized. Taking recognition to higher levels drives performance to higher levels.

Get in the Game

An Off the Bench Leader thrives on giving recognition; they know that reinforcing desirable behaviors drives the climate and builds a great culture. Off the Bench Leaders know that giving thanks fuels fires, creates trust, and turns good intentions into great outcomes. They know that when it's time to change the cadence of the game, to increase the urgency, they will have little problem getting the team on board. All that sincere feedback has built an environment in which they will follow unquestioningly.

Whether you are already in a leadership position or aspiring to one, take some of these action steps right away. You don't have to be in a position of authority to recognize the hard work and success of the people around you.

- Every day, choose someone you want to catch in the act of doing something well; when it happens, recognize them for it on the spot.

- Keep track of your feedback to make sure you are spreading the accolades around evenly.

- Send out a timely group text citing one member of the team for a job well done.

- When someone helps you, especially if they didn't have to, always send a note and include their bosses in the correspondence when possible. Be specific about their contributions and let them know you appreciate the work.

- Always remember calendar events such as administrative professionals day, employee appreciation day, and the like. Your staff will go home and talk about it at the dinner table, and in my experience, they remember those days and how you recognized them longer than almost any others.

- Take a minute for anyone and everyone you see regularly. From the cleaning staff, to the receptionist, to your highest performing team member, notice the people who touch every part of your success. Don't underestimate the value they bring; you may learn something that surprises or even changes you.

COACH'S CORNER

- Remember life is a team experience.

- Every day, recognize and reward the behaviors you want to see in your team.

- Saying thank you is free but it pays you back—big time.

- Be sincere. People can sense your true intentions.

- When possible, raise the stakes by offering a prize everyone wants to win.

Chapter 13

ELEVATE YOUR TEAM: BE THE SPARK

Doing what is expected just gets you to zero.
Give a little better than your best effort every day;
you will be amazed at how much you accomplish.
You are the leader, so lead. Call your own plays.

Every person I've ever coached needed tough love once in while. There's nothing like a dose of reality in the form of a well-placed outburst, but how often can we control the timing of our outbursts and make sure they're appropriately timed? In the long run, coaches with the ability to influence their teams have a greater effect than those ruling with an iron hand or through angry rants.

Thankfully, this was a lesson I learned early in my career. It came from one of the most overachieving teams I ever taught, which also happened to be my first. A few of the girls felt enough trust to approach me, and it changed the way I did things. I was a tough coach at the beginning, yelling, barking orders, and expecting nothing but perfection on each and every play. I didn't have time to influence them; I was too busy trying to lay down the law.

The players at Catholic Central High School played through

all of my mistakes as I was learning how to lead. I slowly realized that fear didn't get people to work any harder, or cause them to want to work *for me*, over the long term. But influence, through reward and recognition, led to a mutual trust and a feeling of team unity, which in turn led to a successful season.

I witnessed this principle in action beautifully at ODU through a conversation Marianne Stanley had with Nancy Lieberman. We had just ended our first season with a loss to North Carolina State in the regional finals in the final seconds of the game. It came down to the ball being in the wrong player's hands at the determinate time.

Nancy was a power forward and high scorer from the beginning. When the going got tough, one way or another and if at all possible, Nancy always ended up with the ball. She was more than capable of delivering, but the team had come to rely on her too heavily; their own development and ability to come through under pressure had suffered in the wake. Marianne and I hatched a plan. What if Nancy played point guard, lower her scoring opportunities in order to move the ball around our very talented team?

Marianne was to have the conversation with Nancy. As head coach, she could have simply said, "You are playing point guard." (As a side note, in 1980, having someone at five-foot-eleven play point would have made us appear crazy. But we had a plan, one that would elevate the entire team.) Instead of laying down the law, Marianne engaged Nancy in the process, laying out the business case—how less on her part would mean more for everyone. Nancy was nothing if not a team player; she agreed to the change in her position for the good of the team. And was it ever the right decision: Nancy went on to become a three time All-American, and the team went on to win two national championships. It helped define Nancy's and Marianne's careers, and it stands as one of the best examples of influence over authority I have ever experienced. Don't underestimate the power of influence.

Bring Everyone Along

When I was first promoted to VP, I was handpicked due to my success in California to head up Central Florida, an underperforming region and a group in need of total transformation. In my entire career, this was my most challenging task. How do you elevate a team who has come to believe they belong at the bottom?

While I had the title and authority to lay down the law and dictate a plan for success, I took another path. Experience had taught me to bring the team along rather than run over them. Over the course of a few days, I got the managers together and announced my intention to reorganize the region. They were tasked with making sure every sales person had an equal opportunity with them, as they could be managing any one of them. Today, no one thinks twice about virtual management, but in 1999 it took some work on my part to convince them they could effectively manage someone outside of their geography. By bringing them into my plan and having them lay out all the details, I influenced the management team to redesign every territory until they believed everyone could win.

At the same time, I influenced each sales person to think of it as open season on territories. I did not tell them where they had to work or on what; I had them tell me. What would their territory be, and what would be their quota? I urged them to be diligent in their research, as whatever they came back with, they would be expected to achieve. As you might remember, the sale associates came back with a quota 33 percent higher than what we were going to be assigned. The management team negotiated the two spaces, the one they designed and the one each sales person requested, to come to me with a final plan. The result? Region of the Year and Board of Directors. Never underestimate the value of bringing everyone along.

Everybody's a Coach…At Least *They* Think So

Back at Catholic Central, at nearly every game I would hear from a particular parent who wanted to tell me how and when to play his daughter. If he didn't talk to me sometime during the game, I knew he'd be calling me shortly after.

After several rounds of this, I asked to speak with him after a game. He agreed, so we met at local coffee shop. Before he could say anything about his daughter, I said to him, "You know that new office on Main Street you are constructing? You need to make the windows a little bit bigger. You should maximize the morning light."

He gave me an odd look and said, "Coach, what do you know about construction and putting up buildings?" I sat for a moment, smiling lightly, then said, "I'm making a point. What do you know about coaching?" I suppose it could have backfired on me, but it didn't. From then on, he trusted me to do my job. He decided to let me call my own plays.

At ODU, it was my turn to execute. We had a leader, and it was my job to get behind her. Yes, we all had a part to play, but make no mistake about it. Though she was a great collaborator and delegator and included her coaches in key decisions, Marianne Stanley called the shots and took responsibility for the outcomes.

Get twelve people in a room, and you'll get twelve different views on how to get something done. As the leader, your challenge is to consider all the data, weigh the input from your team, and then influence everyone to follow one path: your path. In both leadership and coaching, everyone has an opinion. Practically the whole country has an opinion on what the runner-up could have done better in the Super Bowl come Monday. You don't need experience—or even to have ever played the game—to have an opinion. But if you're going to call the plays, you'd better know what you're doing.

At the end of the day, every organization, every team, needs one coach who calls the plays. Once the decision has been made, the team needs to get on board and execute those plays. Company leaders who desire deep benches to cover their growth initiatives really need to get this. Integrate the processes by being open to input and collaboration, but allow one person to call the plays. Make it someone who's been there, someone who has studied the game and walked in the right pair of shoes.

Be the Spark

No one is "on" 365 days a year; that's why a great leader is always prepared to come off the bench to lend heart and hands on those days they are needed. When you lend heart, you boost confidence or motivation; when lending hands, you leverage your own skills and build up theirs.

Elevating your team means keeping a keen focus on what

drives performance. It's about delivering just the right help at just the right time. With the world moving so fast, a leader is like the coach during the single minute between rounds at a boxing match. Time is short and precious, so that leader must be prepared with the right coaching and feedback to elevate the performance in the next round, and in the next, and in the next. It's the timeout in team sports, the pit stop in a car race. Often, it's all we get.

Think about that car race. How the pit crew manages the driver's stops can easily determine who is the first to see the checkered flag. They have to know the car, the driver, and the race well enough to anticipate exactly what is needed and to have all the tools ready to go. During any pause, there exists extraordinary opportunity—to do something great, or to fail spectacularly. Off the Bench Leaders help their teams leverage those breaks to reroute their days, refuel their energy, and guide their interactions as they drive toward the mission. An Off the Bench Leader can change the course and trajectory of a game with a sixty-second message. Is your message ready?

In sports, you practice every day to play the game. In business, you play the game every day and practice…when? It's tricky, if not impossible to find time to practice your craft when you are out there every day doing the job. It can be exhausting, overwhelming, and occasionally frustrating. As a leader, you continually have to come off the bench and add that spark that reenergizes, remotivates, and reteaches your team.

Get in the Game

You are a professional; take the time to learn your products and master your craft. Be knowledgeable about related and intersecting roles and products as well. Become a resource by knowing the whats, wheres, and hows of your company.

Study your trade; know where to go to get things done and how to help others achieve the same.

Keep up to date on current trends and technology. I'm a self-made geek, determined to maximize every useful advance in thinking and technology and to help others do the same.

Coach your people up. Make your passion, innovation, and drive contagious by letting them see you fired up and reaching. Your primary task is to develop a group of people who will go beyond basic expectations, a group that has passion for finding solutions, and a no-options, no-excuses, no-exceptions mind-set. You are creating a group that is innovative and creative and not afraid to challenge the status quo, a collaborative group that works synergistically, setting the tone and pace for their own success.

Clear and open communications drive a successful team. Make every conversation productive. The quality of your conversations will either fuel the team or drain it. Be a fueler.

Just as powerful as writing down your dreams is writing down your formula for being your best self. For me, that means inspiring others. I have an acronym from Billy Donovan, men's basketball coach at the University of Florida, posted in my kitchen, where I see it every day. He takes the word *attitude* and expands it into positive action steps. He references excellence, pride, positivity, and respect, and others. When I sum it up, it's all about being *my* best in order to help others become *their* best, and it's become my touchstone for elevating people. Do you have a touchstone? Find one, or better yet, create your own.

COACH'S CORNER

- Recognize the power of influence. Bring your people along—don't just lay down the law.

- One coach calls the plays. Period.

- Be ready, always, to come off the bench and be the spark that reignites your team.

- Keep learning. Keep improving. Know your business, trade, technology, and team.

Chapter 14

OFF THE BENCH, ONTO SUCCESS

A summary of essential elements for Off the Bench Leading can be summarized in the acronym OFF THE BENCH:

O – Own your destiny
F – Find the best people
F – Focus on development
T – Thank and recognize everyone
H – Have a plan
E – Execute at the highest level
B – Be your best self
E – Enjoy the journey
N – Never settle
C – Call the plays
H – Highlight and review

Let's review each briefly.

Own Your Destiny

Dream big dreams, believe they will be realized, and hang in there during the rough bits. Choose to focus on the positives in your life. Remember, *you own you.*

When you lead, and really all throughout your life, know that in the end, the buck stops with you. Most things in life you have no control over; the one thing you can always control…is you. Your actions, your cadence, and your consistency are all within your power to dictate.

Find the Best People

Recruit the best: the best teams begin with the biggest talent. Interview weekly: make it your mission to never stop looking for talent and promoting your own. Overstaff: build succession plans and always have a pipeline of people ready to fill in at any given moment. Have a deep bench, filled with starters. Remember, talent never goes on vacation; when it's present, it's present.

Focus on Development

To keep people and move them from good to great, or even beyond, create a learning culture. Make sure the mastery of fundamentals is a top priority, and also that every player has a list of personal improvement tasks to work on. If you are fortunate enough to have a team member who has mastered the job, assign them as mentors or offer stretch assignments. Create opportunities for your people to learn in as many different ways as possible.

Thank and Recognize Everyone

Every day, all the time, catch people doing good things and acknowledge them on the spot. Say thank you often to anyone who supports your dream and vision.

Pay attention: discern how your people each like to be recognized. Use different approaches to make sure everyone is included. Have a host of recognition ideas at the ready, both big and small. Everything, from a two-word text to a weekend at a spa, has value when it's sincerely given.

Implement a high-stakes recognition program for job excellence. You can never give too much praise and thanks.

Have a Plan

No great journey gets accomplished with a road map. While dreaming your way to success is important, dreams stay just that if you don't follow them up with purposeful action. Put the preliminary work in and develop a road map to get you where you want to go. Every person on your team and in your organization should have listed goals and a plan for realizing them. Be supportive by reviewing their goals with them regularly.

Remain flexible. The world changes constantly and adjustments are inevitable, so have a plan B, C, and D ready to implement.

Execute at the Highest Level

Without execution, the best-laid plans go to waste. After the planning and preparation, execution requires consistent attention to detail, monitoring, hype, support, development, and most of all, a commitment to excellence. Influence your team to strive for the championship level by living there yourself.

Be Your Best Self

Be true to who you are, and take the hurdles and risks necessary to get you where you belong. That is where you'll shine the brightest.

Be trustworthy and relatable, but keep the boundary between buddy and boss well marked.

Live with passion, courage, and gratitude. Research shows over and over again the number-one indicator of job satisfaction is the relationship an individual has with his or her boss, so be your best self every day.

Enjoy the Journey

Life is so short, it simply doesn't make sense to spend it doing things that make you unhappy. Be bold enough to pursue the job you dream of. If you are not having fun or feeling fulfilled, move on. If you can't move on just yet, pour yourself into building solid relationships with your coworkers. A number of people looking back at the end of their careers have shared with me that single biggest regret was not investing in friendships and having a little fun with the people they spent so many hours, days, weeks, months, and years of their lives with.

Remember how the old song goes? "Accentuate the positive; eliminate the negative…" Do it. Focusing on all the great things you have is infinitely more rewarding and beneficial than dwelling on what you don't.

Whatever you do, balance your life. There will be seasons when work takes a bigger chunk than your personal life, but don't make the mistake of forgetting about the people and pursuits you love. Love really is the point of it all, after all.

Never Settle

I've heard this said many times, and I hold it as truth: "What God wants to give us is always far better than what we want Him to give us." What this says to me is we should never settle for less than the best life has to give us. We only see today. Never give up on your goals, because you really don't know what's coming around the corner.

I could have easily just stayed where I was at any point in my life, but that would have been settling. As a basketball coach, I couldn't have imagined this career in business. Who knew that a coach who went to the University of Hawaii to find out if he really had what it took, and to chase a dream of completely reshaping a program, would years later find himself back in Hawaii, this time to lead a brand-new sales office? You just don't know what's around the corner. Even as a leadership executive, I couldn't have dreamed I'd be putting the finishing touches on a book about all I've learned by leading off the bench.

Never decide to be "done." Keep reinventing yourself. Keep working toward your goals and creating new ones.

Call the Plays

You are a leader. You've earned the role, paid your dues, laid all the groundwork. You know your business. Others will share their opinions, some informed and valid, some neither. Just remember, at the end of the day, one coach calls the plays. In the heat of the game, I would never have stood for an assistant or an AD jumping into my role and calling out plays. Neither should you. I'll say it again, you own you. Have confidence in your plan, the preparation you've done for yourself and your team, and in your own excellence.

There will always be disruptions in the economy. The way people do business is likely to keep changing rapidly. You can't predict what will happen with certainty, but because you're off the bench, you can have a pretty good idea. So go ahead. Call the plays.

Off the Bench Leaders collaborate and connect with their people; they earn the right to challenge and push them beyond what they thought was possible. It is our job to unleash potential; it's the only way to achieve extraordinary results.

Highlight and Review

We've discussed how quickly life moves, how quickly a month, quarter, or even a career goes by. Mark your progress. Remember to check in with yourself on a regular basis. Plan at the beginning of every day, and review at the end. Highlight key areas of accomplishment and also areas for improvement.

Small victories happen all the time, and ultimately pave the way to the big ones you and your team are shooting for. Celebrate! Sometimes making a big deal out of a small thing is just what is needed. And when those big victories come, and they will, raise the roof.

Get Off the Bench

Just in case you've missed it thus far, I'm passionate about Off the Bench Leading. It isn't just about leadership skills, but life skills. You can apply these principles in every part of your life. Off the Bench Leading is not difficult to master, nor is it rocket science. But it is rocket *fuel* for those who aspire to be better than their best selves. It's time. Get off the bench and lead.

ABOUT THE AUTHOR

Jerry Busone is a leadership development executive for a Fortune 500 company, but most people just call him Coach. Jerry began his career as a women's basketball coach, going to the national tournament nine times with three trips to the Final Four and winning two national championships. In 1990 Jerry pursued a career in business, turning around and building up struggling teams, winning twelve performance awards in fifteen years. Jerry has his bachelor's degree in business administration with a master's degree in education. His certifications include Miller Heiman Selling; ICCU Coach; Ken Blanchard's Situational Leadership; Covey's 5 Choices to Extraordinary Productivity; Certified Coach for Gallup's StrengthsFinder; Crucial Conversations; Dale Carnegie Sales Leadership; Franklin Covey's Time Management Keynote and Motivational Speaking; Sales Negotiations Strategies; Leadership Development, Pipeline Management, and Succession Planning. After living in twelve states around the USA and traveling to five continents, Jerry makes his home on the East Coast.

Contact Jerry for speaking, workshops, summits, or coaching at:

www.offthebenchleadership.com

Keynote titles include:

– Off the Bench: A Guide to Being Better than Your Best Self

– Nothing is Impossible, Make It Count

– You Own U: Delivering a World-class Experience to Those You Lead

– Forget the Competition: Pick Your Fight with 2nd Place

– Five Steps to Sales Leadership Success

– Customized topics from the book that you may find helpful for your team

Topics for workshop, summits, and coaching include:

Sales and Marketing • Strategic Planning • Training and Development • Sales Training • Leadership Training • Team Building • Performance Management • Off the Bench Leading • Motivation and Inspiration • Change Management • Channel Development

ACKNOWLEDGEMENTS

There are many people who contributed to this style of leadership called Off the Bench. I don't have the space to mention everyone who contributed, but you know who you are. Here are some special mentions:

First and foremost, David Sluka, Stephanie Sample, and Carlton Garborg at BroadStreet Publishing. You truly are dream makers; you took the concept—my stories and scribbles—and brought it life. You never wavered in your faith in me. *Off the Bench Leadership* is here because of you. Thank you.

Don Bassett and Marianne Stanley. As I began my coaching career, Don was my first true mentor. It was his leadership and dedication that gave me the framework for my success. He would spend countless hours on a Friday or Saturday night teaching me the Xs and Os, the nuances and plays that ultimately led to a national championship. I owe him, and will never forget what he did for me.

Marianne gave me the opportunity and laid the foundation for what I would become. Her wisdom was well beyond her years as a coach and person. It was priceless to have someone like her believe in me, inspire me, and help make my dreams come true. I can never repay Marianne for the journey she allowed me to take with her and the ODU Lady Monarchs.

Jim Jarrett, the best AD a person could ever know. At my long-overdue visit to ODU, he acknowledged my contributions to the program; it was a day I will never forget. Thanks for the opportunity to learn, make mistakes, and grow.

To Karen Barefoot and Nancy Lieberman, who got me back involved with ODU. I am forever grateful to you for bringing me back into the family.

To Mike Marino, my son-in-law. I meant what I said; I couldn't be prouder of you. You and Carly complement each other.

Ed and Rae Nishioka, my best friends. You are there for me even though we are miles apart.

All the kids who played for me and the people who supported me at Catholic Central High School, ODU, University of Hawaii, and UNLV. Thanks for allowing me to learn and grow.

To the media, especially Jim Ducibella, for being so fair to me during my coaching days.

To my ADP family, the greatest—and I mean greatest—organization I've ever worked for. I live for and love ADP every day. Thanks to everyone who has touched my career; I wouldn't be where I am without you.

Thanks To Bob Rathbun, Philip Busone, Mike Kupiec, Mitchell Touart, ,Bob Whittemore, Paul Silitzkey, Darell Nickerson, Jason Maxwell, and Anthony Tavolacci.

To Angelique Sweeney, Dave Cannici, Amy Annee, and Ken Powell. Ken, you gave me the courage and insight to complete this.

Lynne Ritter and Amy Freshman, thanks for believing in me.

To my LDE team, Chris Burley, Chuck Marcouiller, Ken Polk, April Jacob, Chris Blackburn, Maria Sweeney, Nancy

Petersen, Bonnie Danelli, and Bridget Penney. Thanks for the support, encouragement and input.

My emerging leader and new leader classes, workshops, and summit participants. I love watching you come off the bench. Thanks for your inspiration.

NOTES

Chapter 2

1. "US Life Expectancy Ranks 26th in the World, OECD Report Shows" *Huffington Post,* November 21, 2013, http://www.huffingtonpost.com/2013/11/21 /us-life-expectancy-oecd_n_4317367.html.

2. Jeanne Meister, "Job Hopping Is the 'New Normal' for Millennials: Three Ways to Prevent a Human Resource Nightmare", *Forbes,* August 14, 2012, http:// www.forbes.com/sites/jeannemeister/2012/08/14/job-hopping-is-the-new -normal-for-millennials-three-ways-to-prevent-a-human-resource-nightmare/.

Chapter 8

1. Carolyn Schneider, personal message to author, February 24, 2014.

Chapter 9

1. Dave Cannici, personal email to author, June 12, 2014.
2. Ibid.

Chapter 10

1. April Jacob, personal email to author, June 15, 2014.

Chapter 11

1. Ken Polk, personal email to author, May 30, 2014.
2. Marianne Williamson, *A Return to Love: Reflections on the Principles of "A Course in Miracles"* (New York: HarperOne, 1996), 190.